SOCIAL WORK VALUES IN AN AGE OF DISCONTENT

Ann Elizabeth Neely
May 14, 1896 — October 31, 1966

ANN ELIZABETH NEELY MEMORIAL LECTURES

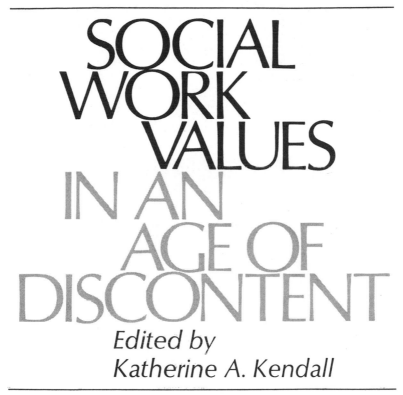

SOCIAL WORK VALUES IN AN AGE OF DISCONTENT

Edited by
Katherine A. Kendall

COUNCIL ON SOCIAL WORK EDUCATION
345 East 46th Street   New York, N. Y. 10017

Table
of
Contents

PREFACE

THIS volume is a memorial to Ann Elizabeth Neely, a beloved member of the staff of the Council on Social Work Education from its establishment in 1952 until her retirement in 1964. The volume has been made possible by contributions from her many friends, who wished to honor her memory through a series of lectures on subjects that were of interest and concern to her. The lectures were given over a period of three years at the Annual Program Meetings of the Council on Social Work Education and at annual forums of the National Conference on Social Welfare. They are now collected in this publication which not only reflects the interests of Ann Elizabeth Neely but, indeed, captures many of the major issues of our times.

The Council expresses appreciation to all of Betty's friends who participated in this effort. Particular thanks are due the Organizing Committee, which created the Ann Elizabeth Neely Memorial Fund, and the Lecture Committee, which planned the lecture series. The two committees, organized shortly after Miss Neely's death in 1966, were led by colleagues who were closely associated with her in work and friendship during her years at the Council—Katherine A. Kendall as Chairman of the Organizing Committee and Ernest F. Witte as Chairman of the Lecture Committee.

Members of the Organizing Committee included Margaret E. Adams, Betty H. Anderson, Emanuel Berlatsky, Edmund G. Burbank, Ethlyn Christensen, Helen Rowe, and, *ex offico*, Ernest F. Witte. The Lecture Committee consisted of Margaret Griffiths, Elsie Harper, Donald Howard, Dorothea Spellman, and, *ex officio*, Katherine A. Kendall.

Special mention must also be made of the guidance received from Miss Neely's close friend, Elsie Harper, in planning the series and preparing the publication. We are particularly happy to have her warm personal remembrance as the opening chapter of the memorial volume.

Katherine Kendall served as editor of the volume. Dr. Kendall's long friendship with Miss Neely, her experience and leadership in social work education, and her skill as an editor made her uniquely suited to this task.

The Council considers it a special privilege to publish this volume. It is our hope that it will adequately convey the deep regard and respect in which all who knew her hold the memory of Ann Elizabeth Neely.

> Arnulf M. Pins
> *Executive Director*

August, 1970

A PERSONAL REMEMBRANCE

Elsie D. Harper

A GREAT deal is known about the professional life of Ann Elizabeth Neely, but less is probably known of her early days and home life. Born in 1896 in Philadelphia, she was the only daughter of William Kennedy Neely and Elizabeth Neely. She had two brothers, one older and one younger, to both of whom she was greatly attached. She attended the Philadelphia schools and in 1916 she entered Cornell University, was elected a member of Phi Beta Kappa and received her B.A. degree in 1919.

She entered the University of Chicago in 1921 and took her master's degree in sociology in 1923. Returning to Cornell University, she became Assistant to the Dean of Women, Dr. Georgia White, until 1927.

A trip around the world took Betty to India, where she stayed for some time at Vellore Medical College, before proceeding to China, Japan, the Middle East, and Europe. These travels made a lasting impression upon Betty. Undoubtedly they laid the foundation for her great concern for all men and women, her interest in international social work, and especially her compassion for the burdens under which so many live and work. She kept this interest and compassion to the end of her life.

There followed a year at Bryn Mawr College. There, as a Caroline Woerishofer Scholar in the School of Economy and Social Research, she studied under Dr. Susan Kingsbury and Dr. Mildred Fairchild.

In 1929, after returning to the University of Chicago as a Kent Fellow with a grant from the National Council on Religion in Higher Education, she completed the course requirements for the Ph.D. in sociology. She was also head of Kelly Hall, one of the University's residences for women.

In 1930 Betty was invited to become executive director of the Department of Personnel and Training of the National Board of the Young Women's Christian Association. During the 18 years in which she held this position and which covered the period of the Great Depression, she found it contained many learnings for her which she was to carry into future realms of work. In the YWCA she supervised a large professional staff and, besides working on setting up of employment policies for the national and local YWCAs, she was instrumental in designing and implementing patterns and standards of professional education. She helped to develop leaders among young business and industrial women, many of whom were black, through conferences, councils, committees, etc. She came to understand the power of group experiences and played an active role in organizing the American Association for the Study of Group Work, later to become the American Association of Group Workers.

During World War II she acted as chairman of the Personnel Committee of the National Agencies making up the United Services Organization, and she was a moving force in developing personnel standards and recruitment policies which were adopted by all member agencies of the U.S.O.

In 1949 Betty became associate executive secretary of the American Association of Schools of Social Work. She delighted in that particular piece of work and once more was able to use the skills she had acquired in the YWCA and U.S.O., especially during the transition period when the Association became the Council on Social Work Education. As a staff member of the Council until 1964, she and her colleagues drew up curriculum guidelines, set standards for the admission of students to schools of social work, established criteria for advanced study, and thus widened the acceptance of social work as a profession.

One of her chief roles in the Council was her responsibility for organizing the Annual Program Meetings. A close associate says these meetings always reflected the breadth of her interest, her capacity to enlist the most creative talent possible, and her flexibility in encouraging experimentation toward making the meetings ever more useful. He continued: "She was undoubtedly the best creator of good public relations the Council ever had, and with her it was a by-product of her living the values she professed as a social worker."

As an officer of the National Conference of Social Welfare and an active member of the International Conference of Social Work, Betty was in the forefront of national and international movements in social welfare. In the year before her death she worked part-time for both the International Association of Schools of Social Work and the U.S. Committee for the International Conference of Social Work. She also furthered good international relations as a member of the Advisory Committee of Atlantique for the selection and exchange of French and American social workers.

Some of us who lived closely with Betty in New York, as Lucy Carner and I did for three years, will always remember her as an individual of many interests other than those which she enjoyed in her professional life. She loved her family first of all and those within the family circle to an extraordinary degree. She gave herself to her friends, to their joys and their sorrows, almost too generously for her health's sake. She read widely, she loved the theatre, music, and poetry, the quiet countryside, and the big old family summer house "at the shore," where she entertained many from the different staffs of the organizations with which she was associated.

Later on, in a small place known as "The Little House" in northern Westchester, she enjoyed the dogwoods and other flowering trees with which its garden abounded, the tulips and daffodils which she had helped to plant, the summer flowers, and the brilliant autumn foliage. She loved to watch the neighborhood children in their brightly colored snow suits, who, when the snows came, coasted down the hill at the side of the house. She was devoted to the ginger cat, who became an important part of the home.

Those who knew Betty best—her friends, her neighbors, and her colleagues—say she made a generous investment of herself in service to her fellow men. We are aware that this paid many dividends, for as she loved people, they too loved her. She was steadfast in her personal relationships. In finishing a given piece of work she sought no self-aggrandisement, though as a good workman she was always happy to receive appreciation for a job well done.

Most of all she will be remembered for her gallant spirit which enabled her to rise above physical handicaps, for the way in which she faced three serious operations in three successive years, and finally for the willingness and serenity with which at the end she chose not to accept invalidism and instead faced the prospect of death.

A British colleague wrote from London: "I recall so many acts that were big in their significance—the simple but tremendously reassuring words she spoke to me when she heard I was to have the same treatment for my sight that she had gone through previously— her quiet support in connection with the International Conference of Social Work." Another good friend, following the 1966 International Congress of Schools of Social Work, wrote from England: "It is grand to think she went in the full flood of activity and with all the flags flying as she would have wished."

Finally, on All Saints' Eve, the day upon which Betty died, one of her most intimate friends wrote: "She was far from a stained glass window saint, but surely she belongs to the glorious company."

CHANGING VALUES IN SOCIAL WORK

*Mitchell I. Ginsberg**

I T IS an honor and privilege to present the first of the Betty Neely
memorial lectures. All of us who knew Betty were better because
of that contact. Her contribution to every part of our profession,
particularly to the Council on Social Work Education, was substantial
and very meaningful.

I was fortunate enough to have had more than ordinary contact
with Betty because we were members of what came to be known as
the "Group Work Club." Group work of 25 years ago did not occupy
the most exalted position in the family of social work and social
work education. The "club" used to meet regularly and try to work
out some of our problems and develop some strength in the group
work sequence. Betty was the unifying factor. And as these years
have gone by, I think each of us has increasingly come to understand
what she meant to that group and to the profession.

I would also like to pay tribute, today, to John Gardner, who—
very unfortunately from my point of view—resigned yesterday as

*Mr. Ginsberg was commissioner, Human Resources Administration, New York City,
at the time of the lecture. He is now dean of the Columbia University School of
Social Work in New York City.

Secretary of the Department of Health, Education, and Welfare. We and the things we believe in and the people whom we are committed to serve have all suffered a serious loss in the departure of John Gardner. Gardner is a man who cares. He brought to his job, in a quiet way, a passion for quality and even for excellence. He offered leadership and that's a rare enough quality. But he also offered distinction, a quality that is perhaps even rarer, particularly in our government. I think all of us are poorer today because of John Gardner's resignation.

Doubt and Uncertainty

In approaching the assignment that has been given to me, I have honestly had some difficulty, but not because the subject or the title didn't leave me sufficient latitude. You will quickly notice that I have not felt bound by the title that was assigned. However, I have felt deep reluctance to approach the subject in a way that would be defined as just another attack on social work and social workers. That is easy to do. It happens all the time. And I have been troubled from time to time by the fact that we, as social workers, all too often seem to enjoy the attack and to relish it. I hope I don't have to say to a group like this that I am proud of my profession, which has given me a good deal of satisfaction for almost 30 years.

The week before I was sworn in as Welfare Commissioner, in New York City, I kept hearing on the radio that a 50-year-old sociologist had been appointed to the Lindsay cabinet. I objected to that characterization, as I said at the swearing in, on two counts. The constant emphasis on a 50-year-old in an administration that is noted for youth seemed to me to be drawing a somewhat invidious comparison. And the term sociologist was one to which I objected; not because I disapprove of that profession, but because I'm a social worker. I'm proud of it. And that's what I expect to be for as long as I'm involved in this or any other position.

And so, from that personal framework, I'm going to try to talk a little about some aspects of social change; in particular about the relevance of social work and social work education to what I see happening in the world—particularly in our country—today.

My comments are largely personal in nature rather than scholarly or completely objective. They come out of the experience of these

14

last two years. It is a fair criticism of me, I think, that as a result of this experience I may have lost some sense of perspective. My hope is that in the time to come, I will perhaps be able to look back at these years with more objectivity.

However, at this time I must say that I find myself in a period of great doubt and uncertainty, both personally and professionally. I often admire those who are so sure about what is wrong and what has to be done, and what other people ought to do. The world of the last two years has been a very different one for me. It's been different not only in degree but in kind. The range of problems, the types of difficulties, the kinds of alternatives that one grapples with are very broad, both in their nature and in their range. Again and again I have found myself having to make decisions without really knowing very much about the real factors involved; without having an opportunity of weighing, in any systematic way, the alternatives. But I've had to make decisions quickly. I've had to make them knowing, sometimes, that the margin of error is very narrow and that the error can indeed have serious consequences.

When you look at the Department of Social Services or the Human Resources Administration in New York, or their equivalents in other cities, you find that the picture looks different from the inside than it did from the Columbia University School of Social Work, or from some other vantage point. A year and a half ago at Texas, when I was making a speech on a somewhat different subject, during a discussion period somebody asked: "If you had to sum up this experience in one word, what would you say?" I thought my usual ten seconds, and then said: "I think I would sum it up in the word LONELY, because that's how I find the job." I don't say that because I am sorry for myself. All of the time I try to remember two things: nobody ever forced me to take the job, and nobody forces me to stay.

One does find in a major administrative post that the time comes when you have to make a decision and make it alone, because that's the only way you can administer a department.

When the day comes that I leave this job, I will never again make the same kinds of speeches that I used to make. I was a full charter member of that club that used to stand up and say: "Why don't they do this today, and what's the matter with them? How come a week's gone by and nothing happened?"

15

I'm not suggesting for a moment that those of us who administer jobs in public services should in any way be immune from criticism and attack. Criticism can be useful and helpful. I would not want it lost. I see very little danger, by the way, that it *will* be lost. But I will say that one can have, or at least I had, the tendency to speak somewhat glibly and with absolute certainty about what other people ought to do.

I have come to know that the alternatives an administrator faces are much more limited than we would like to think. The choices are more narrow and the power is by no means what is often assumed. And I would take it beyond the role of a commissioner and administrator and extend it to the mayor—the mayor of the largest city in the country. It is clear that his power, his ability to make the decisions, to do what he might want to do, is much more circumscribed than I ever assumed to be the case.

Magnitude of Current Problems and Issues

Let me talk a little about my concern about some of the current problem and issues. It is no secret from what I've already said that I am deeply troubled by the situation that this country faces. I'm not alone in that. The United States is facing an enormously complicated and difficult and dangerous time. The term "urban crisis" is badly overworked. But in my judgment, the term, if anything, understates the gravity of the situation we face. The divisions within the country are now greater than they have been at any time, certainly since the Civil War. I see no evidence that there has been a shift in this, or that we are ready to move in the opposite direction. The measures that have been developed up to now to do something about the problems of poverty and ethnic division are completely inadequate. They simply will not work because they do not go anywhere near far enough in the direction that they have to go, nor are they of the nature and scope that will make a dent in the kinds of problems we face.

It is fashionable now to call it the time of "rising expectations" on the part of the poor, on the part of those who have been left out. My experience makes it very clear that this group is no longer prepared to sit quietly by and be left out; to have others make the decisions for them. They want to have something substantial to say

16

about being involved and about the ways in which they are involved. They will demand it and they will not go away.

I have not felt it useful or constructive in these past two years, nor do I feel it now, to talk about the possibilities of riots and disturbances. There is altogether too much talk about the summer—as if it were only a summer problem—and that if you opened play streets and turned on the hydrants and so forth the basic problems of people would go away. Well, they won't. I am not objecting to summer programs, but I am saying that what this country needs are year-round programs—programs of much greater magnitude. If we don't get them, we will have to face the consequences. And the consequences will indeed be serious.

It isn't easy to say as many people do: "Well, there's an extremist group. There are a few militants, and they really don't represent the point of view of substantial numbers of ethnic and social minorities, and poor groups in the country." I don't believe that. Of course, there are differences among them. But the militancy we see is increasing, I believe, and is becoming more widespread and will continue to do so. We would live in a dream world if we simply wrote this off as characteristic of a small group of people.

Inadequate Government Understanding and Response

The tragedy is the lack of understanding and the lack of awareness on the part of the American people. The evidence for that is overwhelming. One need look no further than the President's 1968 State of The Union message. I try not to be too quick and easy in my criticism of public officials. Certainly one ought to feel that way about the President of the United States. But I found that message deeply disturbing. It lacks a sense of urgency, or recognition of the crucial problems of these days and times.

The President talked of some restlessness in the land. He talked about it as a result of the great ship of state taking the waves on the way to a better way of life.

I would not suggest to you, however, that the President is by any means alone in his perception or in what I consider his lack of understanding and awareness. If you listened to that speech you could not avoid being struck both by the response and the lack of response on the part of Congress. When did they cheer? They cheered the President's attack on crime in the streets and what he was going to do about it. In the State of The Union message, he found it necessary, for whatever reasons seemed real to him, to say that he was planning to appoint 100 additional FBI agents and 100 additional prosecutors. I would suggest to you that at this time and with the problems that the nation faces, it is inappropriate for items of that kind to be mentioned in the State of The Union message. And yet, the Congress reacted with overwhelming applause and cheers. To the other somewhat limited statements about the programs which would be of more concern to us, the response of Congress was considerably less than deafening.

How else than through this lack of understanding and awareness can one explain the action of Congress in passing the 1967 social security amendment? I agree with those who say there are good things in it and we ought to take advantage of them. We in New York intend to do just that, but let me say that the good things are in for the wrong reasons. Basically, the problem with this legislation is not just its provisions, as damaging and as hurtful to people as some of them are, but its point of view. I believe this amendment is the most punitive piece of welfare legislation passed in the history of the United States Congress.

But I don't make Congress the villain. That's too easy. I strongly suspect that in passing this type of legislation, Congress reflected the point of view of the American people. Indeed, if one were to submit this, God forbid, to a referendum, I think an overwhelming proportion of the American people would vote for even stiffer legislation against the people who are in our welfare programs.

Inadequate Social Work Response

These things may help to explain to you what I've said—that I do have doubts about the relevance of social work to problems of this kind and of this severity. I recognize, of course, that solutions to these problems do not lie within the capacity, the competence, or the province of any one profession, or even a group of professions. And it is ridiculous and inappropriate to blame social work for these things and for the failures of American society.

Also, it is essential to keep in mind that many members of the profession are making important contributions in many different areas, including services to individuals and groups. Our record in this respect is much better than we give ourselves credit for. We have made a significant contribution in keeping some emphasis on the meaning and the value of the individual in a mass society. This is something that so easily gets lost. Our contribution is an important one in what it does for individuals and as a symbol of concern for individuals. A legitimate case can be made that many people are better off because of what we do.

But then, as a profession, we have claimed more ourselves. We have said we have, and ought to have, a significant role in the social change that is necessary in our society. We have to be willing to be judged not by what we say, but by our performance and our record. I used to say to students in the final class before graduation —it will not be enough to point to your good intentions and the fact that you mean well. That I take, and others will take, for granted. You will have to be judged by how well you perform and you will have to earn the right to a significant role in social change and broad policy considerations. It will not be given to you, nor do you have any right to claim it on that basis. And I think that is true of the whole profession. We have to earn that right. We have to earn that respect. It appears to me that we have thus far not done so.

What is the evidence? For this, let me go briefly through some things and you will note from them the preoccupation that I have mentioned before. It will be no surprise if I start with public welfare: the nature, the scope, the extent of the welfare problem.

Welfare difficulties in the United States are, of course, enormous. A few weeks ago I presented the budget for the next fiscal year for the Department of Social Services in New York. One billion, three hundred and ninety million dollars, just for welfare. With that budget, welfare became the single largest expense item in the New York City budget, surpassing that of the schools. It meant that if the current trend continues—and I must say that there is not the faintest indication that it will not—by the end of the 1968-69 fiscal year there will be over one million people on public welfare in New York City. That is enough to make up perhaps one of the ten or eleven largest cities in the country.

Well, is that our fault? No, of course it's not. But what *is* our fault is the fact that we have not spoken up sufficiently about the inadequacies of welfare and other programs in our urban communities and in the rest of the United States.

I am prone to say that welfare didn't cause this problem. Welfare picks up the casualties of other systems—the failures of education, of employment, of housing; the results of poor health, segregation, and discrimination. The systems fail and we wind up with the result, and then somehow it's our fault that we have all these people on welfare.

Well, how effectively have we made clear the limitations of society's other systems? How effectively have we spoken out about the consequences of these failures? To what extent have we pointed out the inadequacies of the welfare system? While undoubtedly it keeps people alive, basically as a system it has not achieved its objectives and, in my judgment, cannot achieve those objectives.

I am not suggesting that it be scrapped overnight. But to what extent have we spoken up publicly and continuously, made a nuisance of ourselves in pointing out its limitations? At the same time we could have urged improvements in the existing system while opening discussion about possible new systems and possible new approaches.

We have again and again failed to make clear to the American people what we knew all along—that there were millions of people eligible for public welfare in the United States who were not in the program. Had we at least made that clear, perhaps the expansion and growth in public welfare would not have come as a shock to as many people. That would have been our job. Did our profession, including our voluntary agencies, concern itself very much with those millions of people who were eligible, who were in need, but who were not receiving some assistance?

We have accepted the notion that for the social security program one should advertise, and one should recruit. Did it ever occur to us that it might be appropriate to recruit for public assistance when we were talking about people who were in need and eligible? Or are we making the same distinction that is so often made between earned and unearned benefits? How much consideration did we give to the concept of entitlement—that people who are poor and eligible had a right to benefits and services?

In the next few months the Supreme Court will make a landmark decision. It will wipe out welfare residency laws in the United States. This will represent one of the great steps forward, a step that we have talked about for many years. But could we not have played a somewhat more active role in the development and the introduction of those cases? Why was it left to other professions to move forward in the areas that were so crucial to us?

And what about the recent court cases dealing with "the man in the house" rule? Who knows better than we do the terrible consequences of this rule for people and how it destroys families? Would it not have been reasonable for us to play a role in developing these cases? I know individuals have done that. I am not speaking of them. I am speaking of us as a profession because I think that it is an important illustration of where, in my judgment, we have fallen down on our responsibilities.

I have already said you cannot blame us for what Congress did with the social security amendment. We spoke against it. Other groups spoke against it, and, by and large, Congress paid no attention to any of us. But would it have made a difference if over these years we had spoken up clearly and forcefully, again and again, about our program, its limitations, and what had to be done? Might we have had some impact on the thinking of the American public, and thus perhaps some influence on what Congress did and didn't do? Did we ever really make clear what the alternatives are, and what the consequences are of the alternative we pick?

As we move from public welfare to programs like model cities and others seeking to deal with basic urban problems, to what extent are we involved? We have a contribution to offer. We know considerably more than most of the groups who are involved in this program. But are we really participating? Have we been asked to participate? And if not, have we volunteered?

Two months ago, when in New York City we were sitting down to develop plans for the model cities program, I suggested to my colleagues from the Mayor's cabinet who had been charged with the responsibility for setting up this program that one source of information ought to be the New York Chapter of the National Association of Social Workers. I remember the silence of my colleagues. And then they said: "Aw, come on, Mitch, we want to get something done." Well, they may have been wrong. But they felt that way. And they are not uninformed nor are they unimportant.

We know that the model cities program, like the urban renewal program, thus far has been more oriented toward buildings than people. Unless we get in on this program—and fight our way in because we will not be invited—then this program will go the same way as the other programs that we have known. Somebody will stand here a year or two from now and say we missed the chance. Why didn't we do something about it?

And then the poverty program. I know many of you are in it in one way or another; but not to the extent that you ought to be, since the poverty program poses a whole series of fundamental issues that will affect us in our profession for years to come.

Have we given sufficient thought to the implications of the community action program? We are officially in favor of community participation but do we know what that means? Do we, in social work education, prepare our students to work with consumers and clients who increasingly want help on *their* terms and in *their* way? And what is that going to do to the professional role? Can we accept the fact, face up to it, and do something about it—that the rules of the game are no longer to be determined by us? From my point of view, there is a good deal of soundness in this and its implications must be faced now.

What does this all mean with respect to the role of the agencies as we have known them? There is increasing discussion, at least in New York City, about the role and relationship of public voluntary agencies. But the discussion really arises from a different set of concerns than those currently expressed. It's not so much "is the public agency going to take over the voluntary agency?" though I hear that; or "is the voluntary agency going to keep the public agency out?" though I hear that, too. They're both wrong.

Role Uncertainty and Insecurity

Uncertainty about role arises more from a sense of insecurity. Neither sector is able to recognize sufficiently that we are facing a revolution in the delivery and provision of social services. Much of the discussion now and much of the anxiety that voluntary and public agencies will express comes, in my judgment, out of a fear that they are about to be taken over—that new groups are rising up to do what they have done.

Let me give an example. Recently, I met with representatives of a major voluntary agency coordinating group who wanted to discuss

22

what the poverty agency was doing with respect to Head Start. They complained that staff was meeting with Head Start parents without involving the directors of the voluntary agencies. "They don't even tell us what is going on," was the complaint's refrain. I had no sooner finished that meeting when I got a telephone call from the head of the parents group. He said: "What right did that group have to meet with you? We didn't give those agencies permission to come down and talk to you." An extreme position, perhaps; but some indication of the fact that a totally different relationship is developing between the consumers of our programs and those of us who have traditionally given the direction and leadership.

Another example: While I was still Director of the Department of Social Services, I received a letter from the head of a community action group in Brooklyn. He said: "Commissioner, your department has just appointed a new director of the welfare center in my area, and you didn't talk to us about it. You didn't consult us about who that person should be."

I vividly remember tossing that letter aside with a quick reaction: "Well, doesn't he know it's a civil service appointment? And besides, what would he know about the qualifications for a center director? Why don't they do what *they* know how to do and we will do what *we* know how to do?"

A few days later I was sitting on an airplane, traveling a long distance and thinking about that letter and about myself. I remembered that just two weeks earlier I had risen in a public hall and said: "In education, the parents of the children should have a voice in many different areas of the program. They should have something to say about who are the principals, and who directs these programs." And then, as I sat on that airplane, I began to wonder: "Well, if that's good for education, why not for welfare?" I came to the conclusion that the difference was that in one case I was talking about the superintendent of schools and in the second case I was talking about myself. And so, when I got back three or four days later, I called in some of my top staff and said: "I'm not going to be here much longer, but this is what I want you to do. In the days to come, we should not be making any appointments of welfare center directors without consultation with the appropriate groups in the community."

The point I am trying to make here is not about the soundness of that particular decision. I happen to think it is sound, but that's not it. It's our own feelings and attitudes I have in mind. My first, quick reaction really was that this is not the clients' business. What I am suggesting to you is that it really *is* their business, and we are going to have to change our own thinking.

We will have to develop an approach which recognizes that our consumers are going to have greater control of the services themselves, and a much larger share in making the decisions.

Turning to the problem of riots and disturbances, what is our role? We're not going to solve those problems; but it *is* a question. Do we know how to work with these people? Do we have some understanding of what drives them and motivates them? Do we know how to sit across from people who, by and large, have come to think they don't have anything more to lose; who are willing to take extreme actions; who do things that don't make sense and are harmful by our point of view; but who feel driven to go in that direction? Do we have the skill, the knowledge and the attitudes which make it possible to work with them, to have some influence?

And what do we do about the non-militant? I have watched with increasing concern, among my own staff members who are not of racial and ethnic minorities, those who now feel themselves insecure, challenged, and threatened, and who themselves want to strike back. Can those of us who are in administrative roles—and those of us who will move into them—find some way to bring these groups together? What else are we doing in social work that is more relevant to today's concerns?

Outmoded Points of View

I'm not going to go through the list of our concepts whose time, by and large, has passed. A long time ago, the basic notion of readiness was a crucial and strong concept. But today people are not going to wait any longer. They may not be *ready* to make decisions by our standards, but they feel they *have* to make them. They have to make mistakes and learn from them. We are going to have to live with that, trying to mitigate perhaps, but understanding what is involved.

I think of some of the points of view we have traditionally professed. I've spent a lot of time in the last months thinking about the role of a social worker with respect to the ADC mother—a sensitive subject. By and large the profession took the position that these mothers should stay home, that the best place for them was in the family. They should not be working. And we supported that on the notion that it was best for mothers and children to be together.

I have a somewhat different notion today. It may be wrong, but I came to it over a period of years. To some extent, the position we took did not reflect quite what we said it did, but was indicative of a degree of distrust of mothers on welfare, or of low-income mothers generally. For most of us personally and for our friends who are in middle- or upper-income families, the mother may decide to go to work. Millions and millions of such mothers do. The assumption is that she knows how to make the decision that is best for herself and her children. But if you are on welfare—we don't say it, but again and again we have acted in a way which says it—you really don't know what's best and we will have to decide it for you.

If I have a single principle that operates in my approach to welfare and social services and the human resources, it is that people ought to have freedom of choice. I am completely and unalterably opposed to any coercion of welfare mothers or fathers or anybody else. I am also completely opposed to depriving them of choices. So, I have come in this particular area to feel that mothers must be given a choice. We must make it possible for them to have real alternatives, which means providing certain kinds of programs. Having provided them, if the mother decided to go to work, then we have no right to try to stand in the way.

The notion that if the mother is not working she will be sitting home with her children represents one of the myths of our way of life. Like some of you, I have been in "homes"—and I use that word in quotes—in Bedford-Stuyvesant, and Harlem and the South Bronx, and some of the other poverty areas of New York City and other urban communities. Any mother and kids with an ounce of sense wouldn't be together in that apartment for a minute longer than they had to be. And so, we built this concept on a nonexistent world, on a world with an attractive home where the mother and the kids get together and read to one another by the fire.

Some weeks ago, I sat in a beat-up old room in East Harlem, and a mother from the East Harlem Triangle Association said to me: "Commissioner, you'll never understand something. I just got a job, and my daughter, she is seven years old, came home from school one day and she said to me: 'Mommy, I told the teacher today that you weren't on welfare anymore, that you were working.' And the child said, 'You don't know what a difference that makes!' "

The difference is there because we have in our education system some practices that damage people's dignity and self-respect.

New York City provides free lunches to the children of welfare families. If you're not on welfare you pay thirty-five cents. To ease the administrative problems in some schools at lunch time, the teacher says: "Those of you on welfare, go on the other side of the room." For too long the Department of Welfare permitted that to continue in New York City. We are determined that it will not continue even if it means we have to attack another public agency. I'm not trying to make the Board of Education a scapegoat. I suspect that similar practices are true of all too many agencies. But, again, it is fair to ask what we have done about it. Why have we remained quiet when actions have been taken to destroy the very things that we feel committed to and that we talk so strongly about?

And what about the emphasis that we have placed on services? I'm not against services. I believe in them wholeheartedly. But they will never be an adequate substitute for money. In 1962, we played a major part in selling Congress on something we never should have sold, because we never could deliver. Part of the tragedy of the 1967 social security amendment stems from our actions.

In 1962 we said, if you give us money for services, we will do something about the welfare rolls. We knew we couldn't do that. We knew that wasn't the answer, but we thought "services are valuable and this is the way to get funds." We, and more important than that, the people with whom we work, paid a heavy price for that action. So let us at least be clear as to what the limitations are, what we mean by services, and what they can and cannot do.

Mistakes in Staff Utilization and Training

It will be no secret to you that I think social workers should accept more responsibility for staffing the public services. I know of the failure of the public agencies to use professional staff as effectively as they should. These agencies made serious mistakes in staff utilization, but of whom is that not true? To what extent do we in education really differentiate the training of the person who has spent 20 years in a public agency carrying positions of significant responsibility?

I don't want to generalize; that's too easy. But here's one example. We sent a gifted administrator with many years of experience to a school of social work, and when I saw her the last time, she said: "Commissioner, it's as if I'm a 21-year-old just coming out of college. There isn't any differentiation in the program. I don't know what I'm doing here." Well, that's an indictment. Maybe she's the only one, though I happen not to believe that. But if she is, it's still one too many, and we ought to be doing something about it.

To what extent have we understood and accepted our responsibility to become advocates of strong public services? It is not enough, in this day and age, for those of us who are in the schools or voluntary agencies to say that we're doing a good job in education, or in providing the services of our agency. Because a key function, an indispensable one, is also becoming an advocate of strong and effective public services. They're here to stay, and whether they'll be any good or not is going to depend, to a substantial extent, on the degree to which we are willing to fight for them. So each of you who works in a voluntary agency, in my judgment, has two agencies to work for, because it is the public agency that will continue to carry the basic services for most of the poor people in this country.

I read with interest the report from the Council on Social Work Education prepared by Kurt Reichert about what the schools were doing.[1] They are making some efforts in differentiating roles of staff. I would suggest that unless we do more of this, and unless we play a more significant role in defining the different kinds of jobs and the different kinds of preparations needed, this will be taken over by somebody else. They are likely to do a less effective job than we would do. There is a danger of which we should be aware.

We as a profession went much too far in ruling out an appropriate role for the nonprofessional, for the consumer and the recipient. But there is a danger we can go in exactly the opposite direction and rule out *any* role for the professional. There *is* an appropriate role, and it is our job to help define it and make it possible for professionals to play that role. Otherwise, we will wind up not out of jobs—because there's no danger of that in our profession—but out

[1] "Schools of Social Work and Inner-City Concerns, Racial Problems and Anti-Poverty Activities," *Social Work Education Reporter*, Vol. XVI, No. 1 (March, 1968).

of any position to have influence and to exercise leadership in what so desperately has to be done.

We need to make our social workers more knowledgeable about what the basic public systems are, and how they work. It is the public housing agencies, the health departments, the welfare departments, and other services that largely determine the way of life for most of the poor people in this country. To some extent, poor people are affected more by administrative regulations than by the legal system. Do we know enough? Are we involved enough in helping people make effective use of these systems? Do we help them make connections? Do we help them understand what their rights are? And, do we step in and intervene when they are being deprived of their rights, as they are again and again in our system?

An HEW official told me not so long ago of a study conducted by the Welfare Administration. An analysis was done of how people fare in our public assistance system. Do they tend to be taken advantage of? When mistakes are made, in whose favor are they? Well, the results were very interesting. In the adult categories—the aged, the disabled, the respectable poor—errors tended to be in favor of the recipient. But in the ADC program, in the home relief program, errors were overwhelmingly in favor of the agency. That could be coincidence. But I don't believe it for a moment.

So, that is part of our job—to make these systems more honest, to make them more meaningful to the people that we and the systems are committed to serve.

New Roles for Social Workers

In the days to come, the role of the social worker is going to change more and more. The 1970's and 80's and the years to come are going to require a social worker who is much more a generalist and much less a specialist. He is going to have to be more of a supervisor, consultant, evaluator, researcher, administrator. We may not like this. We may decry the lessened emphasis on direct service, but I think that's the way it's going to go. And I personally happen to believe that in terms of needs of this society and our people, that is the way it ought to go.

We are going to have to put more emphasis on evaluation, research, and development. I've been running, if that's the word, an

28

operation that spends over a billion dollars a year, and we have no money for research and development. Can you imagine any other business in this country with a budget anywhere near that size operating in a condition like that? We operate often without having the faintest idea of the effectiveness or lack of effectiveness of the things we do. And we as a profession have contributed to that. We have not been called to task as to whether what we're doing makes a difference or not.

In this area, we have lived a charmed life. We have had a privileged sanctuary. No one has asked us to demonstrate our effectiveness. To an amazing degree, we have been taken on faith. That day is coming to an end and I welcome it. We will have to be judged by how we produce. It is true that measures of effectiveness are difficult to determine, but in my judgment, that no longer will be a satisfactory excuse.

We and our students will have to be much more sophisticated about political, social, and economic factors. Problems are enormously complex. Decisions are extremely difficult. We are developing information systems: electronic data processing; programming, planning, and budget systems; new tools, new concepts. They are coming into our field, and they should come in, because they offer the hope of better service and better ways of meeting the needs of people.

We have to recognize that it is difficult for every one of us that our choices and our alternatives are all so limited. I am struggling at the moment with some of my colleagues on the decision as to whether New York City should go into the food stamp program. It is an enormously complicated and, in some ways, a tormenting decision. On the one hand it would add significantly to the food supply of people—for several hundred thousand people on welfare. On the other hand, it does add to the stigma of people on welfare. And many clients themselves bitterly oppose it on those grounds. I have been advised by some of my former colleagues that food stamps would be a mistake. What I ought to do, they say, is see that all clients get a 25 percent increase in the welfare benefits and therefore solve both problems. I agree. But unfortunately, the alternatives I face are the food stamp plan or the surplus food plan. Those are the choices. I don't have the third alternative.

Given such limitations, where do we go from here? I do not

know. It's much easier to outline my doubts, my hesitations. I have suggested a few things I think we ought to do. I am not by nature, I think, an optimist. And so I must say that I'm pessimistic, or at least doubtful, about whether we can make the changes essential to make the difference.

We have to be aware that unfortunately many of the people in places of power and influence in this country do not put much weight on what we think, on what we feel, on what we believe. I am sure you all experience this. If I may become personal again: time and time again, Mayor Lindsay and Sargent Shriver have made quite derogatory comments in front of me about social workers. These are men of stature and concern. And when I say: "Cut it out," they say: "Oh, come on, Mitch, we don't mean you. We never think of you as a social worker." Well, nothing, I think, annoys me more than that, and I say that to them.

But that's how they see it. They define social work as something reprehensible or, at the very best, not meaningful in terms of the reality of the needs of today. This is a damaging indictment. Too often, it seems to me, we are seen as necessary evils rather than as a profession that could make a significant contribution.

Our point of view and what we have to offer is not sought nor valued by those who are in a position to make the big decisions. What better illustration do we need than the recent discussions on the reorganization of the Welfare Administration in the Department of Health, Education, and Welfare? No change is more fundamental to our concerns. Many individuals and groups were consulted about those changes. Some individuals listening to this lecture were included. But as a profession, we were not significantly involved.

Those of us who are active in the professional association have come to understand the increasing doubts among many of our members as to what we can and can't do, at least in New York. In other cities splinter groups have been set up around the problems of civil rights, peace, and so forth. Members of these groups have come to believe that the association as such doesn't care, is not involved, is not likely to have any significant role.

We have to decide first of all, what do we want to be? What do we want to do? What part do we want to play? There's no certainty that if we do this, our newly defined role will then be accepted. But at least we will know what we want and can fight for it. If we decide against an expanded role, and we legitimately could—Okay! But let's stop kidding ourselves about it. Then some us who perhaps would take a different view could concentrate on trying to pursue those concerns in some different channel.

The Road to More Effective Involvement

All of us have to get into this. We all have to do something about education in the areas that I've talked about—the differentiation of the program, the definition of different roles, the preparation for different roles—not to do the whole job, but to play a part in it. We have to do something about developing a curriculum for the generalist.

We have to do something about our professional organization—who it admits and who it leaves out. In my judgment, it now keeps out altogether too many people who have a contribution to make.

Can we as a profession become more effective in what I have always felt is a key role—developing more communication between those people who are poor and those people who are not poor? Can we at least begin to serve as a possible channel among the disaffected groups in our country who are becoming increasingly disaffected? Is it possible that we can not only listen but begin to hear?

Can we get ourselves more involved in the political arena where, in the end, the decisions are made? Why shouldn't we run for office? Lawyers do, and they get elcted. The evidence of their performance hardly warrants any claim of particular competence in this area. We couldn't do worse. Despite the frustration of these last two years, I would say: "Go into the public services. Accept appointed offices. Get involved." You can be more effective in helping bring about change if you are on the inside.

It always seemed to me that one thing we should have a particular talent for is making the bureaucracy more sensitive to the needs of individuals. That ought to be the contribution the professional social worker in these programs could make as almost nobody else could. Let's get closer to these programs and the public arenas where the decisions are being made.

As I said before, I am not suggesting that we give up our rights to criticize. But at the same time that we're criticizing, let's get in on the programs. Only then can our criticisms begin to have effectiveness and weight.

It won't be easy for us to get in. Nobody will welcome us with open arms. It will be tough. But we have some things going for us. We *do* have a common set of values, a common set of beliefs and ideology. That ought to make it a little easier in the difficult days that lie ahead. We have to be heard. We have to become advocates of what we believe if we really intend to have some influence.

In the end, the decisions will not be made by us nor should they be. In our system of government, the decisions are made in the political arena and the truth of the matter is, I don't know any better way. Winston Churchill once said: "Democracy is the worst form of government except for all the others." And I tend to believe that. So we won't make the decisions. But our responsibility is to be much clearer, much more direct about what we think the alternatives and the consequences are.

Alternatives and Their Consequences

I say that again and again because it seems to me so crucial. This country *does* face alternatives. It is a fantastically rich and prosperous country. It has choices and it has to make them. And whatever choices it makes, it will pay a cost because there are consequences. Can we make it clear what the alternatives are, what the consequences are?

As a nation, we may decide to go the way we've been going. This last year we spent 15 million dollars on public roads. We're spending 6 billion on space, we've spent 3 billion, conservatively, on a supersonic airplane that I'm told cannot fly over the land of this country because of the noise. It will cut off a couple of hours going to Europe, where we are not supposed to go anyway. And we have spent better than 60 billion on defense in Vietnam and God knows where else today and tomorrow. I happen to think most of those decisions are the wrong decisions. But if this country makes them, it will pay a price in other ways; and to what extent have we spoken up about it and said, these are the consequences if you go that way.

We have to speak up. We have to make our position clear. I don't know whether they'll listen. I don't know whether they'll believe us. I don't know whether they'll write the truth. Somebody once said: "The supply of truth is always very limited, but even so, the supply is greater than the demand."

So we have no guarantee as to what will happen. But what choice, what alternatives do we have? I think I know what Betty Neely would say, because she used to say it to me: "Okay, so what do we do about it?"

About four years ago—and I wind up with this story because I remember telling it to Betty—I made a trip at the request of the Office of Economic Opportunity into the Appalachian part of this country to examine the effectiveness of some of their programs. I went into southeastern Kentucky. At what was then Idlewild, I got on, by chance, a new Boeing 727. It was a shining new airplane—it turned out to be its first trip, and it had the smell of a new automobile. By coincidence, on that same day, the *New York Times'* front page was covered with a half-dozen pictures of the moon, taken by one of our satellites. I marvelled at what a fantastic country this is, how gifted are our scientists and how nothing is beyond the capacity, the ability of the United States.

An hour and a half later, I landed in Cincinnati, where a car was waiting for me. In another couple of hours, we were in eastern Kentucky where, in a jeep, I visited some of the hollows in the back woods.

A hollow is where people live, if you want to use that term— exist is more appropriate. You go in a jeep, because there is no other way of getting there. We passed a bunch of shacks, to give them a respectable name. I went to an old schoolhouse built by WPA, the best thing in that hollow, except for the people. There were four young volunteers, two VISTA's and two Appalachian volunteers, who were working that summer, trying to do something under horribly difficult conditions with the youngsters.

I asked them how things were going. They said: "Kind of tough. We have a hard time getting these youngsters into the schoolhouse, so we went from shack to shack, and we talked to the parents, and finally got the children to come. We did some work with them, and all of a sudden they stopped coming. We couldn't understand it. So we went back to their homes and found out it was a part of what we were doing in the schoolhouse. We were using the globe of the world to teach geography. And the parents, when they heard about it, wouldn't let the children come because they didn't believe the world was round."

In the course of seven or eight hours in this one country of ours, I had passed from the world of the bright, shiny jet craft and pictures of the moon to a part of our country with people so deprived, so without hope that you couldn't teach them the earth is round.

I remember that I walked out of that schoolhouse and got into the jeep. And then a young girl, a young volunteer came running out. She caught up to me and I got out and she said: "Dean, is there really any hope?" And I didn't know how to answer her that day.

I'm not sure I know how to answer today. I think there has to be hope. But that, I suppose, is more belief, more because I want to feel that way. But I do believe that if there is hope for that little hollow and for the rest of the country, and for the world, it's going to depend upon a lot of people like each one of us here, and a lot of millions of others. It depends on what we are going to do about it, what we are going to invest, whether we are going to make the difficult, complicated, and demanding choices that I think are so desperately needed.

SOCIAL
VALUES
AND
SOCIAL WORK
EDUCATION

*Robin Huws Jones**

R ECENTLY there has been a good deal of discussion about values
in social work, but the subject, though compelling, even com-
manding, is also elusive. As you follow the argument, it is aston-
ishing how quickly it seems to move away from values and concen-
trates on, well, almost on ships and sealing wax and certainly on
social work methods; on current challenges to the social work profession; on career structures and, needless to say, on student protest.
These subjects are, of course, relevant because, one way or another,
they illustrate this dominant concern with social values. But the
dominance is recent and we ought to ask why.

A man's values are like his kidneys; he rarely knows he has any
until they are upset. Values become significant when they are challenged, when we find other people asserting in Birmingham, Ala-

*Robin Huws Jones is principal of the National Institute for Social Work Training,
London, England.

bama, or Birmingham, England, that their incompatible values are good and (particularly hard to take) that ours are evil. This is especially challenging when our professional training appears to defend their right to hold these different values. Perhaps the most painful moment is when events force us to ask whether there are *any* secure bases for our values or whether all morals are relative, whether the code of virtue we hold, the currency with which we have won affection and respect from parents, teachers, and colleagues, is now devalued or even false. It is then that we look for moral axioms and ask anxiously: are there *any* values that are universal, eternal, and ultimate?

This was one of the significant themes at the 1968 Congress of the International Association of Schools of Social Work in Helsinki.[1] In any society values attract attention when they are changing rapidly, when the conflict of values no longer seems contained but suddenly erupts. We are at such a moment of time today because of convergent revolutions: in the speed of communication, in the control of death and birth, in techniques of persuasion, in methods of destruction, in the revolution in the attitudes that the generations have to one another and toward the supernatural, and the revolution in our understanding of how people behave and how they feel and what they value.

I am looking for reasons why social work education is so concerned with values at present. One other reason which forced itself upon us at the Helsinki Conference is this: social work has given the impression that it is more concerned to reconcile the nonconformist individual to prevailing social conditions and expectations and less concerned to reform social conditions and adjust social expectations. At the Helsinki Congress Gunnar Myrdal denounced social work as an unsatisfactory substitute for social reform and the question recurred in discussion groups: does the social work profession defend the dominant values in society or do social workers in practice often support people in opposition to prevailing values? This is a disagreeable question partly because there is no simple answer; it is an offensive question for it will not stay silent.

---

[1] International Association of Schools of Social Work, "Proceedings of the XIVth International Congress of Schools of Social Work, Helsinki, Finland, 1968," *International Social Work*, Vol. XII, No. 1 (1969), pp. 1-90. See the "Proceedings" for all subsequent references to the Helsinki or 1968 Congress of Schools of Social Work.

Meaning of Values

It is hard to think about values partly because of the difficulty of knowing what we mean by the term. Values, said Roland Warren, are like centrifugal force; we believe it exists because otherwise we can't account for the data.[2] But *our* data are much more difficult to measure or present in such a way that different observers can agree on what they are discussing. By their very nature, values are asserted but they resist examination; they are affirmed but rarely tested—and this is an important lead for the teacher whose job it is to examine and test and encourage his students to do the same.

Muriel Pumphrey describes values as formulations of professed behavior, accompanied by strong feelings.[3] This professing of values and the feelings about them may be passionate, although on examination the values may prove to be shibboleths or myth values. These are the values which a society will parade and pay lip service to, even the ultimate lip service of swallowing them whole. But it will resist as impious any attempt to examine what they mean or consider which other values would have to be sacrificed to gain them. Examples are not hard to find: liberty, equality, and fraternity; the Four Freedoms; dare we ask whether the United Nations' Declaration of Human Rights comes in this category?

These myth values are perhaps not necessarily useless. Gunnar Myrdal spoke of "the equality doctrine" as an ideological force influencing human striving in some measure. In short, although people esteem some values for other people and not for themselves, such valuations are not altogether to be despised; like hypocrisy, they are part of the tribute that vice pays to virtue.

But the proof of the value is in the striving; in the demonstration of its influence on behavior. The essential problem in values—as in economics—is the choice between alternatives; the values that prevail are by definition those for which an individual or a society will sacrifice other values.

What are the characteristics of the *demonstrated* values, for

---

2 Roland L. Warren, "Overview of the Intercultural Seminar," *An Intercultural Exploration: Universals and Differences in Social Work Values, Functions and Practice* (New York: Council on Social Work Education, 1967), p. 72. All subsequent references to the "Hawaii Seminar" come from this report.

3 Muriel W. Pumphrey, *The Teaching of Values and Ethics in Social Work Education* (New York: Council on Social Work Education, 1959).

which people will sacrifice other values, even life itself? The answer is easy, enviably easy, if we can say they derive from an accepted authority, from God, from God's regent, from a party line, or from the authority of 'King and Country,' though even then people choose which commandments to take seriously and which to ignore. Apart from acknowledged authority, values derive their power from influences that individuals no longer recall. People also seek to justify their values in terms of their presumed utility, though utility in this area is not easy to demonstrate and perhaps we have not sufficiently sought for demonstrations.

One reason why the search for universal values is so baffling is that values are seldom revealed except when they conflict. If a value is universal we should hardly know it is there; breathing is seldom thought of as a value.

At the Seminar in Hawaii, Herman Stein suggested there were few values that they at the Seminar could accept as universal, aside from respect for the dignity and integrity of the individual human being. I suggest that it is the business of social work educators to question even this; not to prove it to their students but to encourage their students to try to disprove it. Social workers must—as an axiom —act with dignity and integrity to all human beings. But to claim that all human beings have dignity and integrity is to invite the comment quoted by Lilian Bye in her Report for the Helsinki Congress. She spoke of social work students protesting against words that have 'no real meaning,' words with 'no practical foundation.'

If students of social work are asked to think about respect for the dignity and integrity of the individual human being as literally a universal, they will, I hope, challenge what is meant by respect, dignity, and integrity in this context, and by universal. These values *may* be 'universal' in one's own group, defined by national boundaries, race, ideology, or whatever; but those outside this group may be treated consistently as something less than human. Again, in what way can we respect the dignity and integrity of individuals—sometimes in positions of power—who are besotted with cruelty? The great man or woman may feel compassion for "the pity of it," but we have to justify our use of the words 'respect,' 'integrity,' and 'dignity.' Our lively students are likely to go further and ask about protracted vegetative existence in extreme senility, about infants born with severe physical and mental handicaps. These topics are still not often discussed in public though doctors and others will talk about them in private. Sir Theodore Fox, lately editor of the *Lancet,* was brave enough to deliver a lecture on the theme that it is not always a doctor's duty to prolong life.

I am not now trying to argue for any one view on these hard questions. I am arguing the difficulty of achieving any precise statement of what even this value, "respect for the dignity and the integrity of the individual," means in practice. The point, and it is almost banal to make it, is that our students—and we—grow in understanding by searching out these difficulties rather than by glossing over them. Roger Wilson at the Helsinki Congress suggested that we should try to see why the issues are so complex, indeed insoluble, in the hope that this will enable us to live more courageously with conflicts.

If we insist on searching for some universal value here, perhaps we may find it in that capacity that men have, and have so generally that exceptions could be pathological—the capacity to value some people highly, even to the point of sacrificing other values for them. What differs is the radius of the group that a man values highly; on the one hand, the group may be confined to the small circle of family or friends; on the other hand, it may encompass humanity.

The Values of Social Work

What about values in the social work profession itself? Professions presume common values; they are one chief link binding members of a profession together. Professional values imply a consistent choice prevailing, it is claimed, over the lesser values of income, power, and prestige. Serious departure from these values carries with it the threat of excommunication.

The seminar at Hawaii considered those values that underpin the social work profession. These values are articulated slowly; they are not yet altogether formalized, codified, or established. They arise out of the problems that characteristically present themselves in practice, problems such as confidentiality, self-determination, and what one writer has called 'impersonal justice,' doing your best for the client no matter how you may be feeling or how tiresome he may be.

A few empirical studies have been published on this topic, including one thoughtful and careful piece of work by McLeod and

Meyer.[4] This study (limited in size and location) supports the hypo-thesis than social workers are to some small extent distinguished by certain professed value position. These values appear to be related to training but almost equally powerful is the influence of religion—or lack of it. Social workers with no religion and those of Jewish faith rated high in the values that distinguished social workers. It was found also that the value positions of social workers, as conveyed in the tests used here, differ from those of, for example, teachers. The conclusions are all tentative—except the recommendation for further research!

It is always tempting on an occasion like this for a speaker to say what *he* thinks should be the lodestar, the essential axioms of the profession. At Helsinki, Myrdal put *equality* forward as the desirable universal value of all professions concerned with making social policy or with carrying it out. It seems a pity for me to miss the opportunity to plug one or two candidates for consideration; one I believe to be central for social work educators is *objectivity,* respect for evidence, what some people are old-fashioned enough to call 'truth,' the determination to test our hypotheses by rigorously trying to disprove them. I believe this value is useful; I esteem it as a value all the more because it is *not* universal. Perhaps the most terrible words in the whole of Hitler's *Mein Kampf* are those in which he determines to purge from the souls of the German youth what he calls "this taint of objectivity."

In social work education—and in social work—I think we tend to take another essential value for granted; it might prove sharper and more effective if we did not. It is hard to find a fresh phrase or bright, particular words to convey this value. The words that come to mind make us feel a little uncomfortable, like 'compassion' or, as the Quakers put it, 'concern.' Traditionally, social work is concerned for the neglected, the nuisances, the uninteresting hopeless, the less eligible. Traditionally, I said, but not consistently. And when this traditional value falters we should beware, for the leaven goes and leaves the lump.

One of the special hazards of the social work profession arises from the clash of values that is likely to exist between a social worker

[4] D. L. McLeod and Henry J. Meyer, "A Study of the Values of Social Workers," *Behavioral Science for Social Workers,* Edwin J. Thomas, ed. (New York: Collier-Macmillan, 1967), pp. 401–417.

and his client when it comes to what Pumphrey has called "the process of responsible decision-making."[5] It is said that the social worker's job is to help clients face the facts of the choice and see what is likely to follow from this choice for themselves and others, but that the social workers should avoid saying or implying what the client ought to decide.

Among other writers, the philosopher Dorothy Emmet suggests that this may not be valid. "Social work," she says, "seems to me to have built into it . . . some sort of aim which, if not purely a moral aim, at any rate has a strongly moral ingredient in it."[6] She argues that if a client is to achieve a measure of integration within a community, it means coming to terms with some of the dominant norms; it means bringing his moral ideas into sufficient harmony with those of other people so as not to be in conflict with them all the time. Let me add that integration here may—and often should—mean adjusting the society as well as adjusting the individual.

English history records an official called the Keeper of the King's Conscience. It must have been a hot seat! Today there is, I suspect, a tendency to make social workers the keepers of society's conscience. In Britain it is alarming in debates in Parliament to hear it taken for granted that stubborn social problems would be solved if only we had more social workers, solved by reforming the nuisances and the threatening characters, but leaving everything else comfortably as it is. The social worker's job is to reconcile the needs of society and of the deviant individuals; in this he must beware especially when he is highly esteemed by the establishment.

These days we can never get away from this polarity: the reforming role of social work on the one hand and on the other hand the treatment role which helps individuals adjust to society or, as it is more aggressively described, "social work as an agent of social control."

Social work was condemned by Myrdal at Helsinki as an unsatisfactory substitute for social reform and social policy. The form of this attack, we may think, was not particulary informed nor pro-

---

5 Pumphrey, *op. cit.*

6 Dorothy Emmet, "Ethics and the Social Worker," *Social Work and Social Values: Readings in Social Work,* Vol. III, compiled by Eileen L. Younghusband, D.B.E. (London: George Allen & Unwin, Ltd., 1967), pp. 11–21. See also articles by Florence Hollis and F. R. Kluckhorn.

found. But it went along with what some social workers and students said in their National Reports to the Congress and in the discussion groups. This also was part of Mitchell Ginsberg's message in his paper on "Changing Values in Social Work."[7]

On the other hand, community workers are uncomfortably aware, in technically advanced countries no less than in the developing countries, that social workers can be attacked by the establishment, by those who control the budgets, when they, the social workers, highlight the slums and the ghettos, condemn poor schools, inadequate medical services, bad working conditions, inconsiderate administration, and other deficiencies in their communities. Social caseworkers, too, are condemned when they challenge society's right to impose some of its prevailing values by punitive means. In Britain in this context one recent debate has been about homosexuality, another has been about abortion.

But this is the nature of social work; it is one of the risks we assume when we become social workers. If we do our job with competence, we are pretty sure to be shot at by one side or the other, except, of course, when we are shot at by both.

The Challenge to Social Work Education

What is the upshot for social work education? We must begin, of course, where the students are and today students are likely to exhibit two conflicting attitudes; if they are good, they will insist on challenging everything, including their own commitment and what they think their teachers represent. At the same time, they will be 'hot for certainties,' hungry for some firm axioms, for some stronghold sure.

The aim of social work is to produce effective social workers capable of further growth, men and women who earn their keep in terms of the help they give to individuals, groups, communities, and society with social difficulties that can't be solved unaided. We know far too little about what sort of education produces the effective social worker and this question cries out for more empirical study. If, for instance, we teach the relativity of values, the doubtfulness of clear decisions, do we produce social workers less able to help their clients effectively? And yet the relativity of values must be taught

---

7 *Supra,* pp. 11-32.

42

not just between cultures but in a single culture, even in a single person. Values are not fixed points but part of a continuum; they constitute part of what Kluckhorn calls "value orientates." Circumstances affect their form and stability just as H_2O represents water only within given limits of temperature and other conditions. The teacher has to engage his students in a dialogue about whether there are any literally absolute values or whether in practice *all* require interpretation—unless, of course, we are rigidly bound by the letter of a tribal law and not by the human spirit.

This is the teacher's dilemma and his challenge. No longer can he try to convey a stable and reliable value system and then help his students reconcile this with the conflicting values of some of his clients. The task is to see the relativity of value systems: that what is universal is the existence of values rather than this value or that, and then he must help them find some way "to live more courageously with conflicts." The problem is how to equip students whose work is carried on "in a setting of unresolved social, administrative, and moral conflicts," with a competence in handling just these value conflicts.

Would it be fair to say that to a great extent schools of social work in all countries meet this challenge by simply dodging it? Pumphrey stated that values were not explicitly taught or discussed in schools of social work in the United States. This, of course, is true of professions generally; it is the exceptional medical school that seriously discusses the ethics of medicine and I have met very few doctors who have actually taken or even read the Hippocratic oath. We expect these professional values to be *conveyed*, especially by the patterns of excellence students meet in their training. Professional values are learned in the way described by a plumber who was asked how he taught his apprentice. "Well," he said, "he hangs round till he catches it"; 'hanging round' is an essential ingredient in learning, but it is not enough.

If they are given an opportunity, and sometimes even if they are not, our better students are prepared to sharpen their tools by worrying their teachers about the values their society holds. As we know, today they will attack all sacred cows and may even assume that whatever is sacred is likely to prove a cow in disguise. Why, just why, for ordinary people, for the poor, and for minority groups is democracy really a better system than communism? Why is truth

SOCIAL WORK VALUES ON THE NEW FRONTIERS

"O, Beautiful for Pilgrim's feet, whose stern impassioned stress
A thoroughfare for freedom beat across the wilderness . . .
"America, America, God shed his grace on thee
And crown thy good with brotherhood from sea to shining sea"
(Katherine Lee Bates, America the Beautiful)

In these few lines are summed up some of the most compelling and persistent themes of American life: the stern, tight-lipped, driving discipline of Puritan ethos; the beckoning wilderness—the frontier existing but to be conquered; the struggle to keep open the paths of individual freedom; the expectation of a special meritorious relationship with God. The boastfulness, achievement, myth, and self-satisfaction are all there. It is descriptive of a vast do-it-yourself program except that it assigns to God the responsibility for the crowning gift of brotherhood.

---

*Ruby Pernell is a professor at the School of Applied Social Sciences, Case Western Reserve University, Cleveland, Ohio.

From time to time in our history we have been confronted with the painful fact that not only freedom, but brotherhood, too, was our own, not God's responsibility. The outpourings of initiative and enterprise which have characterized American growth have been and still are much more easily directed towards the mastery and extension of our physical and biological world than to the world of human relationships; throughout our history one frontier after another has been breasted and the new territory beyond revealed, only to become a new target for conquest. Our physical frontiers are now somewhere in outer space. In biological sciences we are seeking the keys to creation and eternal life, as men once sought them through religion. In man's relationships with his fellow man, however, we remain, as it were, in barricaded settlements as timid newcomers on the edge of a vast, undeveloped, hostile land. Indeed, the wilderness is encroaching on what was thought to be cleared land. The creeping undergrowth and hanging fringes of moss are reclaiming their own. This is the true frontier of our times, resisting piecemeal attacks with inadequate tools, unbacked by sufficient will or courage to forge ahead. Despite the oratory of patriotic days, our good has not yet been crowned with brotherhood.

The Puritan Ethic

The Puritan's code of conduct and action was peculiarly suited to the task he set himself, of conquering a strange, unknown, hostile land. As geographic and economic expansionist opportunities for a long time seemed unlimited, it is no wonder that his brand of ethics became the indelible mark on those who followed him to these shores and went beyond through the wilderness, working, fighting, destroying, and cheating their ways across the continent.

Tawney said of the Puritan,

> He drew from his idealization of personal responsibility a theory of individual rights, which, secularized and generalized, was to be among the most potent explosives that the world has known. He drew from it also a scale of ethical values, in which the traditional scheme of Christian virtues was almost exactly reversed, and which, since he was above all things practical, he carried as a dynamic into the routine of business and political life.

[1] R. A. Tawney, "Economic Virtues and Prescriptions for Poverty," in *Social Perspectives on Behavior,* Stein and Cloward, eds. (Glencoe, Ill.: The Free Press, 1958), p. 267.

The frontiers which stood before him in America presented the opportunity to continue the space exploration started by his voyage across the ocean and unfinished as yet. The frontier life demanded and repaid the individual initiative and unceasing toil and beckoned toward greater returns for those who would brave the hostile wilderness.

To quote Tawney again,

> Limitless increase and expansion . . . production . . . systematic and methodical accumulation . . . won the meed of praise that belongs to the good and faithful servant. The shrewd, calculating commercialism which tries all human relations by pecuniary standards, the acquisitiveness which cannot rest while there are competitors to be conquered or profits to be won, the love of social power and hunger for economic gain—these irrepressible appetites had evoked from time immemorial the warnings and denunciations of saints and sages. Plunged in the cleansing waters of later Puritanism, the qualities which less enlightened ages had denounced as social vices emerged as economic virtues. They emerged as moral virtues as well. For the world exists not to be enjoyed but to be conquered.[2]

And so men hacked their ways forward with social and moral sanction for their self-seeking behavior. The creed, severed from its religious base, is still with us as an everyday reality, still potent in the beliefs of those who succeed, still used as the screen through which to view the unsuccessful. But this set of values, proven so effective in clearing a way through physical, biological, and economic barriers, have in themselves created a host of problems in man's relationship with man.

Exploitation of Minorities

It would seem that the concept of brotherhood has always been difficult for Americans. John Steinbeck, in his book *America and Americans,* comments in his pithy style:

> The whole thing is crazy. Every single man in our emerging country was out for himself against all others—for his safety, his profit, his future. . . .[3]

The self-interest, the economic opportunities, and the social and moral sanction for exploitation of resources led inevitably not only

[2] *Ibid,* p. 276.

[3] John Steinbeck, *America and Americans* (New York: Viking Press, 1966), pp. 14-15.

to use and abuse of land and capital but of human beings as well. The destruction of the great forests were nothing as compared to the destruction of the Indians and their culture; the stripping of minerals from the earth nothing as compared to the stripping of culture and manhood from the black men brought as slaves; and on the newer frontiers of urban life and growing industrialization, the exploitation of men, women, and children as productive units was of much less concern than that of overworked farm animals. (In fact, the Society for the Prevention of Cruelty to Children was preceded by the Society for Prevention of Cruelty to Animals.) To use Steinbeck's vivid language again:

> From the first we have treated our minorities abominably. . . . All that was required to release this mechanism of oppression and sadism was that the newcomers be meek, poor, weak in numbers and unprotected—although it helped if their skin, hair, eyes were different and they spoke some language other than English or worshipped in some church other than Protestant. The Pilgrim fathers took out after the Catholics, and both clobbered the Jews. The Irish had their turn running the gauntlet, and after them the Germans, the Poles, the Slovaks, the Italians, the Hindus, the Chinese, the Japanese, the Filipinos, the Mexicans. . . . The turn against each group continued until it became sound, solvent, self-defensive and economically anonymous—where upon each group joined with the older boys and charged down on the newer ones.[4]

It only seems just that at this point in history the blacks, browns, and reds should be using the same mechanism against the white, Anglo-Saxon protestants. If we are going to be full members in the same club, then everybody—even the first comers—ought to be initiated.

Social Responsibility and Self-Righteous Values

In a society conceiving of itself as "Christian," where there is both the opportunity for socio-economic mobility and a sanctioned ruthlessness in human relations, somebody has to be the keeper of the Good. Someone has to care about safeguarding humanitarian values against predators. Someone has to be the other—rather than self-oriented. In our history these have been the humanitarians, the social workers, the social reformers. Fortunately, the same religious sources from which the puritan ethic was derived also provided con-

---

4 *Ibid*, pp. 14–15.

cepts of responsibility for the welfare of one's "brothers," while the pioneer communities of freedom-seeking men, newly formed in a new land, also provided a growth milieu for norms expressive of the interdependence motif of the collective moral and social values. Religious, philosophical, and political thought contributed to the development of a "social conscience," motivating not only acts of charity but of justice.

However, our major problem has been that the services and institutions growing out of the social responsibility—social conscience motivations have never quite been able to escape the entwinings of the more dominant values of our society. In the same way that the individualistic pursuit of the golden opportunities of expansionist America has been so destructive of human beings and human relations, so the pursuit of the common good has been constantly hampered by this righteously self-centered system of beliefs. While we give with the right hand to the poor, the unfortunate victims of the system, we manage in some fashion to deprive them with the left. The system of social work values—which in their basic generalizations embody the best of the humanistic beliefs of man's intrinsic worth, his potential, his right to make his own decisions, his rightful place within the community of men and the responsibilities that the community of men have toward him—nevertheless is infiltrated at the operational level by those same sternly punitive, rejecting, prejudiced views of the Puritan. We are caught in our own myths, firmly believing in the land of golden opportunity and just as firmly not believing in the man who hasn't made the most of it. As individuals we will give to the United Fund or even vote for civil rights, but we rush home to barricade ourselves in the suburbs against a possible advent of even one poor or black person.

Social Work and the Social Good

At this crossroads of competing values stands the social worker with a double historical task of urging movement toward the social good and rescuing those who have been lost or trampled on in the mass competitive rush towards personal affluence and social upgrading. The social worker ideally represents the social conscience of the community, prompting us toward action in keeping with our highest ideals; and the collectives of social workers should function in the same way in relation to their most earthbound members.

In the past the social worker was obvious, easily spotted in proverbial hat, gloves, and flat heels, going about "doing good," secure in her moral aims, and in the knowledge of a community of similarly secure fellow-workers. But now, in this season of our discontent, the social workers' faith in each other is shaken or lost. The normative behavior, goals, ethics, and values are being questioned by the young and the black and those who make common cause with them. The question is "is social work (practice, values, organization, agencies, etc.) relevant to today's needs?" There is no one correct answer; in fact, each questioner is likely to have his own answer ready before *asking* the question. We are too often like the student who undertook an inquiry on relevancy, stating, "In order to substantiate my point of view (which is 'no'), will you please fill out the attached questionnaire."

There is no denying that today is not like yesterday. Every institution of American life does need to examine itself today for "relevancy" and gear itself to change in a rapidly changing world. The question of relevancy addresses itself to the selection of goals and the system of beliefs and explicit values of the institution, the integrity with which these inform every activity, and the utility of the institution in carrying out its social purposes.

American social work, both as an expression and instrument of American moral and social values, is inextricably tied up with what America is at any one period of time and thus tends to reflect the major concerns of the era. We have moved as the times demanded or permitted from a commitment to charity, to a commitment to justice, to a commitment to science. Though lessened in their power as choice determinants, the central motive of each of these periods has been carried forward as increments. Compassion, social justice, and disciplined knowledge are all part of our armamentarium, though we fall short in all three.

To quote John McDowell, writing in the Conference Bulletin,

> The word 'value' is used in the profession of social work to convey a concept . . . to mean 'that standard or principle which leads persons to select one option over another in making day-by-day choices.' It is not what we say but what we do that reveals our value system . . .

> Values pose real choices because they always seem to come in pairs. The choice is seldom between good and evil, but between one good

and another, or between an evil and lesser evil.[5]

Parsons defines values as,

Patterned conceptions of the qualities of meaning of the objects of human experience; by virtue of these qualities, the objects are considered desirable for the evaluating persons. Among such objects is the type of society considered to be good, not only in some abstract sense but also for 'our kind of people.' The value patterns that play a part in controlling action in a society are in the first instance the conceptions of the good type of society to which the members of the society are committed. Such a pattern exists at a very high level of generality, without any specifications of functions, or any level of internal differentiation or particularities of situation.[6]

The idea of what constiutes a "good" society can vary, particularly if it is cast in terms of "our kind of people," which can range in inclusiveness from family to all mankind. Indeed, this inclusiveness as well as exclusiveness is part of our problem, for, in Steinbeck's words, "We speak about The American Way of Life as though it constitutes the ground rules for the governance of heaven" and want to impose it on everyone else.[7] At this level of generality we are talking of values such as democracy, individual freedom, justice for every man, and the common good. These, however, must filter down into an operational level at which they are internalized and institutionalized to give structure and direction to our daily choices of action. In this process a great many values, norms, and motives emanating from the sub-structures and individual conditioning enter the course, and the system sometimes gets out of line with its remoter values. Our most cherished myths lie at the remote ends of these misalignments where we still cling to the value and believe it is directing our choices, while in fact we have departed far from it.

It is important, however, that we continue to cherish the value even when departing from it, because it serves as the goal to turn toward at threatening moments in our history. With slavery, the exploitation of immigrant labor, with civil rights and poverty, the appeal for justice and human rights reaches into the moral realm—

[5] John McDowell, "Guest Editorial," *The Conference Bulletin,* Columbus, National Conference on Social Work, Vol. 72, No. 2 (Winter, 1969), p. 3.

[6] Talcott Parsons, "Youth in the Context of American Society," *The Challenge of Youth,* Erik Erikson, ed. (New York: Anchor Books, 1965).

[7] Steinbeck, *op.* cit., p. 32.

the collective conscience—for a response. Without these values the conscience would remain undisturbed.

Parsons describes the dominant American value pattern in its moral aspects as fundamentally individualistic, maximizing the desirability of individual autonomy and responsibility, and controlled normatively in two ways. First, it is premised on the idea of building the "good life" not only for the individual but for all of mankind— "a life that is considered desirable, not merely desired. This includes commitment to a good society." He goes on to say:

> The society then has a dual meaning, from this moral point of view. On the one hand, it is perhaps the primary field in which valued achievement is possible for the individual. In so far as it facilitates such achievements, the society is a good society (that is, its progressive improvement) is the primary goal of valued action. . . . To the individual therefore, the most important goal to which he can orient himself is a contribution to the good society.[8]

This is, in effect, the value platform on which the social worker (used broadly here to designate the person who devotes himself to activities to improve the social conditions of individuals and the society as a whole) has stood: for himself he sees his major obligation to be his duty to his fellow man, to free him to function; i.e., to free him to make his own contribution to the building of a good society, and to work for those changes in the society which will permit greater individual initiative and autonomy.

The Question of Relevancy of Social Work Values

Now we are questioning the relevancy of our values in today's world. Yet, a reading of the stated goals of those who raise the question indicates the good society and individual autonomy to be the very self-same ends sought. This suggests some mis-connections between our values and our actions. Obviously social work itself must have a number of its own myths whose substantive realities have been corroded over time.

Parsons suggests that "the main pattern of [American] values has been and will probably continue to be stable, but . . . the structure of the society, including its subsystem values at lower levels, has . . . been involved in a rapid and far-reaching process of change."[9] The

---

8 Parsons, *op. cit.,* p. 115.

9 *Ibid,* p. 117.

attempts to cope with the increasing complexity and differentiation in our society, the effects of science and technology, an increasing productivity and pursuit of affluence, rise of ethnic groups into the middle classes, the migratory waves of southern blacks from south to north and of northern whites from inner to outer urban America, have brought into prominence as determinants of choice those social values (as distinct from "moral" values) arising from desirability or expediency. "The common good" can be quite provincially perceived, and "our kind of people" can be taken as the only people who count. The guaranteed annual income may be all right for the farmer who agrees to let his fields lie fallow, because he is "our kind of people"; but a guaranteed annual income for a migrant or tenant family grossly exploited by that farmer is not to be countenanced. They are too common to be included in "the common good."

The social worker and social work institutions, as part of the mainstream of American life, have been caught up in these currents of change, too, so that while the main value pattern—the *raison d'être* —has remained stable, the lower-level values have changed greatly. In the process, some misalignments have occurred. There are two intermingling streams of development we may examine: one, the institutionalization of social work activities, and the other, the ascendance of the "scientific" or "professional" approach.

One of the more frequently referred to historical writings is Porter Lee's 1929 Presidential Address to the National Conference on Social Work on the union of cause and function in social work in which he discussed the current concern that the capacity which social work had shown for upholding and inspiring enthusiasm for a cause should not be lost as it became more of an established and well-organized function of community life.[10] Well, in 1969 it is once again a concern, increasingly so with the growing problems of society, the concomitant demands for services, and the further development of a "professional" who seems more likely to respond to the demands for service than to those for social reform.

The early social workers were generally people who were clear about their mission to help those less fortunate than themselves, to root out social evils, and to rally others of their own class to support the cause. The chief motivation was altruism, and long, irregular

---

[10]Porter Lee, "Social Work: Cause and Function," *Proceedings, National Conference on Social Work* (Chicago: National Conference on Social Work, 1929), pp. 3–20.

hours with little monetary reward were to be expected.

With the social assistance programs of the thirties, social work began to be more of a "job," and then, with the growing development of university schools of social work, a profession. With these changes, other more personal motives entered in: earning a livelihood and occupational status, to mention two which have been of significant influence. Along with this, encouraging and encouraged by the trend, was the development of increasing numbers of organizations to carry on social welfare tasks. We were passing out of what Charlotte Towle referred to as phase one, "the stage in which social workers felt solely responsible passionately to persuade the community to support its good works," and into phase two (still with us), "in which social workers conceive of themselves as employees of the community, responsible to administer the community's good works and subject to its authority in so doing."[11]

Parsons points out that the moral value pattern of our society places heavy responsibility on the individual to help the society toward progressive improvement, but nevertheless subjects him to two crucial sets of limitations. One of these is the fact that individualism is bound within "a strongly emphasized framework of normative order," and that achievement must often be in the context of collective organization, thus limiting autonomy.[12]

For the social worker this means that he must rely on the organization with which he is affiliated to provide the moral conditions which make it possible for him to operate in line with the remoter values to which, hopefully, he subscribes. The misalignment of the organization, thrown off by the prevailing social values and demands at this earthbound level, therefore seriously hampers or completely blocks the potential contribution the individual worker may make to further the "good" society. (This is part of what the young social workers and students today are rebelling against: the institutional restraints on individual autonomy.)

If the institution then can be perceived (however myopically) as an expression of "the community's good works," the worker's identification with it and his acceptance of its authority may possibly

[11]Charlotte Towle, "The Role of Supervision in the Union of Cause and Function in Social Work," *Social Service Review,* Vol. XXXVI, No. 4 (December, 1962), pp. 396–411.

[12]Parsons, *op. cit.,* p. 116.

give him a sense of fulfillment so far as his own value commitments are concerned. But this is not enough, for, as Towle says:

> Although a profession is an expression of the conscience of the community, its own conscience cannot be external. Out of the special knowledge and understanding of the human welfare implications of social conditions a profession is expected to contribute to the development of community conscience. Implicit in its function is the responsibility to foster social welfare causes. . . .[13]

This, then, is a significant part of the problem before us: how to swing the earthbound social welfare institutions into better alignment with our basic values so that the worker within can find the way to make his own contribution to the good society, with the resultant good, not only to those served, but also to the community as it is moved to a higher level of commitment to the common good.

A concurrent stream of development which has contributed to the imperfect connections with our basic values has been the increasing emphasis on a knowledge-based technical skill in the performance of social work. Professionalization, with all its necessary and positive contributions, also has its hazards. The choice and execution of particular theoretical orientations and the elaborations of these into practice can and have led us into exclusiveness, denials of service to those who do not pass certain criteria of "readiness," focus on treatment of individuals, with neglect of attention to the social conditions which spawn the problems, and a general preoccupation with the techniques of making theory work. "Objectivity" and "professionalization" have become cold, negative terms to many present day social workers and students because they conjure up feelings of, to use Towle's phrase, "the emptiness of the informed head divorced from the informed heart."[14] In the heat of this moment in history the "disciplined use of self and knowledge" has lost some of its appeal.

In Varley's illuminating study of social work values of students in two schools of social work, she measured the impact of social work education on four social work values: equal rights, service, psychodynamic-mindedness, and universalism:

> It was assumed that the service value (being primarily other, rather than self-oriented) was part of the foundation upon which social

13Towle, *op. cit.*

14Towle, *op. cit.*

56

work had built its claim as a profession. Therefore, in rendering service, a social worker should limit the relationship to the technical task rather than to subjectivity and personal involvement (universalism), be impartial in giving service to all clients irrespective of personal sentiment (equal rights) and systematically apply a body of knowledge relevant to the client's problems (psychodynamic-mindedness).[15]

Briefly, the study showed "a significant negative change at graduation time on service, psychodynamic-mindedness and universalisms. Only on equal rights was a trend on increasing commitment observed. . . . Graduating students appeared to reject the values of rendering service to clients based on the application of a systematic body of knowledge in a controlled, task-oriented relationship."

As Varley points out, "humanitarian values may appear to conflict with the universal technical task-orientation, or legal values applicable to the rights of social workers may conflict with dedication to service. On the other hand, the scientific values underlying psychodynamic-mindedness may conflict with humanitarian values, or the libertarian values within equal rights may appear to contra-indicate a universalist approach."[16]

This brings us back to the question of relevancy in today's world in which clarion calls are sounding for justice and equality—economic, political, and social, and the zeal of the reformer has risen in the breasts of many. The existing institutions and ways of life seem to stand as barriers between the individual will to do good and the good he feels he could bring about. For a younger generation than those who hold the forts of the Establishment, this is the frontier— the hostile wilderness of demands and forms and requirements interlaced with attitudes which deny human need, dignity, or intelligence; and it is to be attacked with that same, individual initiative, free enterprise, ruthlessness, and righteousness which took the pioneers across the American continent and up the economic ladders to conquest.

Probably nothing bothers the "old-timers" as much as the imputation that they never cared or tried to do anything about poverty or peace or prejudice, that their values have been weighed and

15Barbara K. Varley, "Social Work Values: Changes in Value Commitments of Students from Admission to MSW Graduation," *Journal of Education for Social Work,* Vol. 4, No. 2 (Fall, 1968), pp. 67–76.

16*Ibid.*

found wanting. In their own freshness of youth they, too, were seized with the spirit of reform called forth by the times and are stirred by the call again. The results of a 1966 study of attitudes on social action of members and those in leadership roles in the Chicago Chapter of the National Association of Social Workers in the writer's words "seemed to show greater liberalism than might be expected" on endorsement of an activist role for the chapter.[17] Sixty-six percent of the leaders in the sample were social work administrators or social work educators and 80 percent of the membership sample were caseworkers. In all the social action issues included in the study, the scores were generally on the liberal side for both groups, with the leaders scoring higher than the members. This is heartening news, for it suggests that there are considerable numbers in the ranks and the lieutenancies who are not so irrelevant after all, and who are stirred by the beat of the same drums as the young, fresh troops.

We are each products of our own historical period, and most of us tend to follow or fall in with current developments, while a few emerge as leaders. However, very few people really rise above their times; that is, few have the vision and zeal and power to move forward at a strategic point in history and point the way to a new path. This is what Martin Luther King, Jr., did for America and the troubled conscience of America. For those searching for their own identity and integrity as whole or "real" persons—white or black—a direction appeared. Here, in a social justice cause lay the opportunity to become one's best self. One path to affirmation of self is through an occupational role consistent with one's set of beliefs, which offers the opportunity for expression of those beliefs, through use of one's best skills. For many, then, stirred by indignation over injustice and inequality and the social values which perpetuate these, social work holds out the promise of fulfillment of one's mission. But, as Erikson points out, the evolvement of identity starts with trust and trust must be grounded in integrity.[18] If the newcomers among us are angry because they feel their trust betrayed, then the question is integrity, not relevance, and we must address ourselves to this. Have we strayed

[17]Donald Brieland, "Attitudes on Social Action and NASW Member Participation: A Study of the Chicago Chapter," *NASW News*, Vol. 13, No. 1 (November, 1967), pp. 17–21, 23.

[18]Erik H. Erikson, *Childhood and Society* (New York: Norton, 1964).

in our daily practices so far from our moral value base that, like the Puritans, we are making virtues out of vices? Then let us reform.

Social Work as Cause or Function

If the question is whether we should be disciplined "professionals" and devote our energies to carrying on services, rather than be "reformers" drumming for a cause, I cannot accept the necessity for a choice. Both are undoubtedly required. This is not to say that any specific professional service is to be perpetuated in whatever form or for whatever purpose it is presently given. We do not want to imply, as does the old report of a certain home for unmarried mothers, "how sad it will be if after a hundred years of service this Home has to close down for lack of girls needing help."[19] In a highly complex, heterogeneous, rapidly changing society in a scientific age, it is inconceivable that social and individual problems will disappear with the elimination of poverty or with a new power base for blacks. There are new problems emerging constantly and it takes training, skill, and experience to devise creative means for helping with their solution, and a good deal of just plain drudgery to carry on.

In Brustein's article "The Case for Professionalism," he comments that "The permanent dream of this nation, a dream still to be realized, has been a dream of equal opportunity—the right of each man to discover wherein he might excel."[20] Social work today attracts, and should provide equal opportunity to, two kinds of people whose excellence must complement each other and in each of whom a trace of the other should be discerned: the practitioner and the reformer. Neither plays his role alone; both require a broad public base of support and assistance. Porter Lee though these two roles required different combinations of human qualities and, in a "flight into rhetoric" (his words), he drew this picture:

> The emblazoned banner and the shibboleth for the cause, the program and the manual for the function; devoted sacrifice and the flaming spirit for the cause; fidelity, standards and methods for the function; an embattled host for the cause, an efficient personnel for the function.[21]

---

19 Quoted by Dorothy Emmet in "Ethics and the Social Worker," *British Journal of Psychiatric Social Work,* Vol. VI, No. 4 (1962).

20 Robert Brustein, "The Case for Professionalism," *The New Republic,* Vol. 160, No. 17 (April 26, 1969), pp. 16–18.

21 Lee, *op. cit.*

Fortunately, the picture does not provide such stark contrasts today, although there are many who would have us think so. There are an infinite number of small causes fought daily over the program and the manual to win a little more dignity and respect and life for the people we serve. And this must go on while the big battles are being fought under emblazoned banners, with the help of a larger fellowship of those who care.

> . . . it is not to be wondered at that some persons with the temperament of the prophet rather than that of the executive deplore the preoccupation of social workers with organization, technique, standards and efficiency which have followed the development of social work from cause to function. . . . [But] we cannot meet this challenge by going back to a day when social work was exclusively or predominantly a cause. We must meet it with the sober recognition that it is and must be both cause and function.[22]

I believe the cause must bind us all if we are to have our own validity, our own integrity, and each of us must find our own way to work for it. These are troubling times, and challenges come by the minute to raise question within and among us about what we really believe— what we really value. We value life, we value man's humanity to man, we value respect for man, we value the true dignity that comes to the giver as well as the recipient of respect. We value the gifts that come with the abundant life, but only if these can be shared. We value the "good" society that permits these things to be. If these are not the values we hold and for which we earnestly work, then we shall perish.

In the words of Martin Luther King, Jr.,

> We must work passionately and indefatigably to bridge the gulf between our scientific progress and our moral progress. One of the great problems of mankind is that we suffer from a poverty of spirit which stands in glaring contrast to our scientific and technological abundance. The richer we have become materially, the poorer we have become morally and spiritually.

> Every man lives in two realms, the internal and the external. The internal is that realm of spiritual ends expressed in art, literature, morals and religion. The external is that complex of devices, techniques, mechanisms and instrumentalities by means of which we live. Our problem today is that we have allowed the internal to be-

---

[22] *Ibid.*

come lost in the external. We have allowed the means by which we live to outdistance the ends for which we live. . . .

Our hope for creative living in this world house that we have inherited lies in our ability to re-establish the moral ends of our lives in personal character and social justice. Without this spiritual and moral reawakening we shall destroy ourselves in the misuse of our own instruments.[23]

Perhaps the true, unmastered frontier lies within our own hearts.

---

[23] Martin L. King, Jr., *Where Do We Go From Here: Chaos or Community?* (New York: Harper & Row, 1967), pp. 171 and 173.

A NEW CONCEPT OF RESPONSIBILITY IN SOCIAL RELATIONS

*Eugen Pusic**

THROUGHOUT the history of man it is clear that he needs his fellows for survival and, at the same time, competes with them for survival. This deeply contradictory relationship has determined the basic patterns of human behavior in a way analogous to the mechanism of genetic information regulating biological reproduction. But analogy is not identity. That, possibly, is our best hope for survival in the future, for the inherited social pattern regulating our behavior in society during millenia has actually become dysfunctional. Instead of contributing to survival, it spells the gravest danger for survival. Can we change it before it is too late?

Even if, at present, we know too little for a conclusive answer, let us concentrate upon the question. Popper's saying that cognition begins not with collecting facts or constructing theories, but with problems, is fatefully relevant in our present situation.

*Eugen Pusic is dean of the Advanced School of Public Administration, University of Zagreb, Yugoslavia.

The Power of Uncertainty in Shaping Behavior

The exact nature of the processes in the tissues of the human brain—perception, memory, forgetting—is still largely unknown. The basic mechanism regulating behavior in the individual is, therefore, a matter of conjecture and sometimes simply of metaphor. It is pictured—apart from behavior determined by the genetic code—as a pattern of concentric circles. Expanding circles, when the life-experiences of the individual jell into some sort of residue of increasing generality, or contracting circles, where these residues function as switches orienting the individual's actions in real-life situations in more and more specific ways.

The residues of conditioned reflexes, attitudes, values, beliefs, internalized norms, roles, etc., in the individual are established by associating tension or relief from tension with certain forms of behavior. The more dependable the association in experiences repeated over time, the more stable, in general, the residues. The tensions, which are relieved by appropriate behavior, stem from uncertainties in the natural and social environment of the individual.

It is here that the dilemma starts. Nature cannot be reasoned with. It is fight or flight as for any other animal, and this is the source of deep-set patterns of defense and aggression. The human environment, on the other hand, is a more complex proposition. It can and does appear as nature, as a potential source of danger or of need satisfaction, as the case may be, eliciting the same response of defense and aggression. But, at the same time, it is society, the sheltering and protecting group, the main—in the beginning, really the only—available form of insurance against towering uncertainty. This pressure of pervasive uncertainty is initially the most potent agent of socialization. Acceptance by the group is a condition of physical existence for the individual and he cannot see his existence as separate from the group. His whole life is subject to the rules of group life in a measure which does not permit rational thinking of ends and means to arise. Every action has to be sanctioned by a rule derived from the group. Aggression within the group is as unthinkable as it is normal between groups and in the extra-group environment generally.

In this way, the individual learns to seek relief from tension by two basically incompatible methods: Through defense—aggression in competitive affirmation of his interests—and through conformity—

63

acceptance of the protective security of his group.

These were the basic boundary conditions established for human behavior, and in this framework what we call progress was achieved. But at what price? Lucien Lévy Bruhl, in his *La morale et la science des moeurs,* questions whether in social development there is wastefulness, an unjustified expenditure in suffering, in misfortune, in physical and moral pain, in every generation sacrificing the majority of individuals to the functioning of society as a whole.

Strangely enough, the price is increasing to prohibitive proportions precisely at the moment when the commodity bought for it is becoming less indispensable.

The development of the patterns determining human behavior is characterized by growing complexity. An increasing number of values and norms creates alternatives for the individual. These alternatives are in the beginning experienced as conflict and are so interpreted to the present day by humans conditioned to harmony as the basic condition of social solidarity. Nevertheless, these very conflicts, the choices with which the individual is faced, the order of preference he has to establish for himself, signal the birth of freedom. With the possibility of choice comes perspective. Alternatives create distances and the individual begins to see himself as different from his group, from society generally. Not all rules are necessarily accepted. They are seen as imposed from outside, as stemming from the expectations and requirements of society. As the pressure of uncertainty is reduced, social institutions are developed with the purpose of replacing diffuse environmental pressure with specific social constraints. Power as a peculiar form of concentrating the available instruments of physical violence in a community, of monopolizing the control of sources of uncertainty society-wide comes into being. And though power in all its forms—patriarchal, patrimonial, governmental—tends in the beginning to be absolute and arbitrary, it is no longer completely identical with the individual's own internal programming. However large a part of society's commands and injunctions is internalized through the artifice of reward and punishment at the hands of the powerful, there is at least a remainder which is experienced as being imposed from the outside. And in revolting against this imposition, however mildly, however tentatively, however covertly, man lives his freedom for the first time.

In this sense history is the growth of freedom. The broader the span of requirements, the greater the variety of roles, the more bewildering the diversity of rules, the more confusing the contradiction in values—the better for freedom. The multiplicity of bonds creates choices; all these demands cannot but conflict. Conditioned as he is to accepting conformity, man tends to resent—at least with one side of his personality—this conflict and the freedom it implies. He sees it, in the words of the cautious conservative Durkheim, as *anomie,* the breakdown of security bestowing law and order.

And well he may see this, to an extent or for a time. As long as uncertainty in the environment is not reduced below a certain threshold, there is no substitute for the safety and stability of society. It is this uncertainty which generates the dialectic of emerging curiosity, with erupting activity on the one hand and defensive security and cringing avoidance on the other. In man's development, the fight for freedom and the escape from freedom are not the quaint self-contradiction they are sometimes made out to be. They are simply the consequence of a homeostatic information-processing and decision-making program with originally very narrow boundaries.

But the boundaries are widening. Rising levels of productivity—understood as the ability to satisfy interests of any description—reduce competition for the satisfaction of material needs of existence. Expanding standards of rationality replace emotionally underpinned categorical norms with neutral hypothetical rules derived from the regularities discovered in nature and behavior. Social conformity, therefore, becomes gradually less important both for counteracting the consequences of unbridled competition and for ordering goal-oriented cooperative activity. Modes of both conflict and cooperation subtly change. Emphases shift away from the time-honored social institutions of enforced regulation, the simple binary switchboards where the "yesses" and the "no's" were backed by appropriate rewards and punishments. Of these institutions, one stands out as particularly ominous: the political state. The threatening amplification of power achieved in the modern super-states is particularly frightening because this huge potential is the last form of power which remains basically unregulated. Ultimately, the competition between states is left to the maxims of the jungle.

The information-processing surface which a progressively more complex society provides for the individual is becoming larger. Alternatives of values, dispersed interests, memberships in multiple coalitions—all these contribute to widening the leeway for the individual's orientation. But will he have the courage for his freedom? Will he know how to develop new forms of responsibility to replace the comfortable irresponsibility of obedience? And will he do all this in time?

The Forces That Reduce Uncertainty

What would have to happen in the reality of the world as it is today for these questions to be answered in the affirmative?

There are, first, general preconditions. Uncertainty impinging upon man from his natural and social environment would have to be reduced considerably below the threshold that has been reached by now even in the most developed parts of the world. Let us affirm at the outset that this is technically possible. But it has to be done. And a mere technical possibility, with the prevailing patterns of behavior being what they are, is by no means a certainty.

Technical productivity, that is, the available technological capacity to produce, when fully used and rationally distributed, is sufficient, within a reasonable span of time, to remove economic insecurity, uncertainty as to the satisfaction of basic organic needs, from the face of this planet. The actual achievement of this goal, even if only in a smaller part of the world, is already significantly influencing aspirations, hopes, and the temper of thinking across all frontiers. This most recent stage, when, in normal times, stark organic deprivation no longer constitutes a threat for the majority of members of a community, has been achieved in the greater part of central and northwestern Europe as well as in North America. It has also been achieved, at a lower level of technological sophistication, in most east European countries. This is significant because it demonstrates the margin of productivity within which this achievement is possible for a country by changing the ground-rules of distribution.

Uncertainty stemming from man's natural environment, however, is not the main problem today. The heavy and general pressures come from a social order in which, in Michel Crozier's words, control of the most important sources of uncertainty is still concentrated within comparatively small circles. We are living in power-societies, and the gradients of power—political, economic, organizational, even sometimes patriarchal power—run from the powerless to the powerful. The segregational influence of this stream of power is considerable. It splits society into unequal groups of the governing and the governed, the rich and the poor, the accepted and the tolerated, the honored and the despised. The split may occur along any of the lines of class, race, nationality, religion, or belief which have been used to separate people from each other during our long and painful walk toward humanity. Groups which share unequally in the values and benefits their common environment has to offer must necessarily be antagonistic. The more favorable position of one group can only be based on the relative deprivation of the other. And maintaining society partitioned into antagonistic groups means to preserve much of the social climate of primordial group-society where the relationships of absolute solidarity within the group and absolute hostility between groups created and reinforced the ambivalent patterns of conformity and aggression that bedevil man's journey toward rationality to the present day.

This arrangement of roles and institutions is in the process of disintegrating anyway, at least in the more developed parts of the world. Possibly the process should be speeded up and rationalized. It is important to understand that the reality of supremacy and subjection—however veiled in form and glossed over—has to be removed before even the attempt can be made to change the corresponding patterns of behavior. This means to propagate and make more general the structures which partake of the nature of coalitions. We already have them here, even if only a few and in very rudimentary form. But there exist organizations which, together with parts of their interacting environment, represent coalitions, in the sense that every interest-group, and eventually every individual, engaged in a common undertaking has in principle the same amount of leverage to enforce his particular interest demands. This leverage is based on his usefulness, on the contribution he is making to the joint purpose. The contribution can be positive through his performance, and it can be negative as well through his abstention from interference with the collective operation when he is normally—in a factual and legal sense—in a position to interfere. Most advanced forms of work such as scientific research, higher education, complex engineering designs, and medical and social welfare teamwork is carried on by coalitions that include not only the people actually engaged in the activity but also groups essential for the financing, the placement of orders, the licensing, the review of results, the development of methods, and others. To find out how to generalize this type of framework for working together is one of the most important tasks of—if you will pardon the expression—social engineering, which lies before us.

To weave the network of cooperation out of the strands which now constitute the ropes of power is no mean task and it is hardly possible even to see all the implications. One of them is the reappraisal of the ideology of efficiency. Efficiency, as the demand for maximal rationalization of effort at a comparatively low level of technological development, tries to transform people into parts of a quasi-machine. They must become cogs dependent on each other and ultimately on the purpose of the whole mechanism represented by management. The increase in productivity ascribable to greater efficiency is limited to a short, though very conspicuous, span in the ascending curve of growth. It is the time immediately after industrial revolution when the advantages of a systematic division of labor at the level of the task are manifest but mechanization of work is not yet fully underway. In the longer run, however, the decisive advances in productivity have all been achieved by transferring work to machines, fed by new and more abundant sources of power. It is science and technology that stand at the frontier of progress and not the "one best way" to perform manual work. But then, it is perhaps not too great a price for establishing relationships of coalition-partnership, of equality at work, if we have to face the reduction in the machine-like efficiency of human work. Our productivity is likely to go on increasing even without transforming people into parts of a machine.

And now we come to the really difficult part. For reducing uncertainty to levels where the attempt at changing prevailing behavioral information codes determining individual behavior becomes a practical proposition a third major condition has to be fulfilled. It is to replace the actual international disarray with some semblance of order, and order cannot mean hegemony of one power or a group of powers any more than it can mean world government. Not because that would be impossible—even if it were so today, it might very well become possible at some future time—but because this would mean transferring the problem of power, with which we are faced nowadays in every country individually, to the level of the world. And then it might really become unmanageable. What should be the countervailing mechanisms that could check and balance a worldwide monopoly of the means of physical violence?

We have to construct an international system with a built-in tendency opposite to the iron law of oligarchy, to initiate processes of equalization of influence at the same time that a growing interdependence would limit arbitrariness of decision in any part of the system.

One problem in this context deserves particular attention. The trend towards equalization must be worldwide. No third world, no "wretched of the earth" must be left out if the seeds of violence are to be removed and not only transposed. But the larger part of the world is today at a stage of development when the establishment of stable and effective national power is still a progressive future goal. Normally it should be expected that increase in economic and military capability in these countries will result in more aggressive political attitudes within the national territory as well as in the international arena. How should these countries develop to a more and more equal status with the rest of the world without having to repeat the philogenetic path through aggressive, competitive, national power-societies and without being controlled by a superior outside power? This is a problem which has not even begun to receive a solution.

Here, as well, some indication of possible approaches does exist. But the signs are even more shadowy than the few existing types of coalition at the level of first-line cooperation at work. There are, on the international scene, forms of activity, organizations which, even when they are called "governmental," are essentially independent of power in the performance of their tasks. Their number today is about 2,000; the number of professional people they employ less than 100,000. If these international organizations—from ILO to the World Council of Churches and from the International Olympic Committee to the Red Cross—should number 100,000 and the number of people working for them—not their reputed "members"—should be counted by the tens of millions, maybe we would begin to get somewhere. The network of functional cooperation the world over, where people work at tasks of common interest without depending on organized violence or other forms of imposition, should increase in density, quickly and steeply. There is no other way to displace the competitive jockeying for political power-positions which characterizes the relationships between states then to crowd it out by other forms which would gradually take over all forms of constructive, useful, international interchange and would, by contrast, show more clearly the dangerous, if ludicrous, anachronism of present-day international politics.

Fusion of Social Welfare and Human Rights

If all these are only preconditions, our future may seem to contain little hope. Obviously, the relationship is logical, not chronological. The achievement of more satisfactory directions in the processes of history can be attempted only simultaneously with the corresponding changes in our behavioral information code. And if this should still seem like a tall order, two thoughts are recommended for consideration: (1) We have really no alternative. As long as we are genetically so programmed as to strive for survival we have to go on because there is no other way leading to survival. Karl Marx thought that humanity in its progression tackles at a certain time only those problems which it is able to solve. It is, however, difficult to predict what can be solved and what cannot without having tried. It seems, therefore, a more dependable maxim for action that those tasks, however forbidding, have to be assumed, and cannot be left undone. (2) We do not start from scratch.

Two concepts, still in their gestatory stage, merit our particular attention: First, there is the emergence of human rights as a limitation on the unrestricted possibility of the power holders to please themselves. Traditionally, the notion of right has developed as a regulated relationship between subjects of a power center. Their claim upon the center was at best a claim for protection against the infringement of their rights by other subjects, a claim for arbitration in the case of conflict, and a claim for implementing the settlements as pronounced. The wielders of power themselves were above the rules they imposed on others. From time immemorial they did "as the Senate pleased" and in so doing they could do no wrong in any sense that would be practically relevant within their society.

The first time it was affirmed that the king *could* do wrong, that the ruler was not absolved from obeying the laws he promulgated, a genuine revolution was achieved in the human condition. The changes in the attitudes, the feelings, the acts of man which this reversal of principles effected from the moment it was first proclaimed testifies to the powerful logic inherent in a system of rules. This is true even if these rules—and this is still their main weakness— were not and could ultimately never be enforced within an order where overwhelming force was concentrated precisely in the hands of those against whom the rules embodying human rights should have been enforced.

Second, at the same time the idea of a minimum level of existence guaranteed to the individual by society found expression in a number of new institutions and activities that go under the generic name of welfare in its widest connotation. While human rights were far-reaching in their abstract implications—though in practical life honored mainly in the breach—welfare measures were from the start practical and concrete enough although often woefully inadequate in scope and based on all sorts of antiquated ideologies. While the proponents of human rights were often unable to translate their correct reasoning into reality, the reality of progress, even if small-scale, was achieved by welfare—frequently for the wrong reasons.

From its beginnings, however, welfare functioned independent of power. Real welfare measures very seldom needed enforcing. It is, therefore, significant that most of the successful international large-scale organizations are in the field of welfare in its widest sense. WHO, ILO, UNESCO, UNICEF, FAO can operate on a world-wide basis in health, education, social security, and social work, in child welfare and in the fight against hunger, in most cases without needing any enforcement machinery behind them. This is why they function and produce results far ahead of anything which can be expected of the political machinery of the United Nations.

Given the actual though sporadic protection of human rights and the existing though not universal minimum welfare floor limiting the possible decrease of living standards, some might feel, with Bertrand Russell, that even today aggressive competitive behavior, exhibited nationally and internationally, cannot be accounted for by prevailing pressures of uncertainty alone. Even today the embryonic institutions of equality are ahead of the inherited behavioral drives. If nothing else this discrepancy should point the direction in which we should go: toward stabilizing the new institutional framework, reinforcing the influences which it must exert on values and attitudes.

That would mean, first, to establish minimum standards of welfare as a human right. Such a fusion of the two essential institutions preparing a new society would strengthen both. Welfare should obtain a stable threshold no longer subject to further discussion among any kind of interest groups in society. And this minimum welfare for all is a matter of elementary right, not involving any question of dignity, capability, self-reliance, or any other device developed in order to lower the status of one individual or group in relation to others.

On the other hand, proclaiming the right to welfare would provide a human right with methods of implementation already perfected through years of practical experience in the field of welfare. As a matter of fact, how did welfare succeed in imposing a levy on the powers that be? To begin with, through the threat, real or imagined, which mass destitution spelled for the existing order. But after that the development of general welfare systems mainly had four aspects:

- With the increasing numbers of beneficiaries of welfare services, interests were mobilized which were too strong to be disregarded, let alone slighted.

- The increasingly professional character of welfare work in its many aspects created a powerful and well-organized interest group whose interests to a large extent—in so far as they were not "private practitioners"—coincided with the interests of the beneficiaries in expanding welfare benefits and services. The various professions of welfare have more than once functioned as social action groups in the struggle for progress in welfare.

- Potent existing beliefs and values were enlisted to reinforce the pressure for more welfare. The pertinence of welfare to the ideals of justice, equality, and humanitarianism was established as self-evident.

- Finally, through the existence of a considerable network of nongovernmental carriers of all kinds or through the gradual establishment of organizational forms independent of government, welfare was taken out of the hands of the power establishment. This last achievement can, however, demonstrate its advantages only after minimum standards of general welfare have been adopted and accepted. Therefore, for most of their past history the relations of welfare and government were ambivalent. Under the influence of democratic reforms, government became more responsive to the interest of the masses and was, in this way, sometimes the most important agency in establishing welfare standards. On the other hand, the possibility of misusing welfare for purposes of power was never very remote and remains present whenever welfare is dispensed only or chiefly through agencies closely allied with the centers of power.

The further development of institutions of welfare and of human rights, together with other causes contributing to the reduction in the level of uncertainty, should eventually result in a radical change in the matrices of behavior. This change might be prognostically described as a new concept of responsibility.

In the power societies in which we live, responsibility is based on power and flows from power. It is the principle of obedience to authority, based on the regular experience of punishment for disobedience. This experience is eventually, and optimally, internalized in the form of duty and the dictates of one's own conscience. Immanuel Kant has formulated the corresponding moral rule to act in such a way that the maxim of one's action could be a principle of general government.

In the functional society of the future, responsibility should be different in all its dimensions. It is the expression of a new social relation. Not of submission to the will of others but of cooperation in activities which can only be performed in common, of the necessary mutual respect for the interest-minima of each partner in the interest coalition emerging around the collective activity. In a coalition, each partner adds the weight of his contribution, positive or negative, to the achievement of the common purpose. Respecting his interests is, therefore, not a question of fair play but a condition for the activity to go on.

The Task for Social Work Education

Finally, what is the significance of all this for social work education?

Whatever social work education may become in the decades to come, it is certainly not going to be what it is today. But the certainty of change is not unique to this field. Education generally, assuming paramount importance as the process of self-programming human behavior, cannot remain what it has been: a process of imparting knowledge and conditioning behavior performed by one group of people upon another group. The fundamental premises of this relationship of subjects to objects of the teaching operation are no longer tenable. It is equally obvious that education cannot be limited to any particular part of the life cycle, not only because of the obsolescence of knowledge, but mainly because of the different functions in society, the increasing depth of understanding, the changing emphases in interpersonal relations which a human being can internalize and learn systematically only at given junctures of his progress.

Taking these momentous changes into account for the long run, the question still remains: what are the probable next steps? First, to be able to stand the strain of steeply increasing requirements for elasticity and adaptation, the various professions of welfare—for this is how we think of them when turning to the future—cannot be taught in terms of skills, that is, as some kind of dexterity in handling people based on a few obsolete simplifications about "human nature." Understanding change and social development, a "feel" for the problems inherent in the various development situations cannot be taught at all in the traditional sense. This can be acquired only by the learner autonomously in discussion and observation. We have yet to discover what help from the "learning environment" would be optimal for speeding up this process. In the most progressive forms of education in the field we are just beginning to find our way toward these new learning communities—but to know does not always mean to know really, especially if the implications of new knowledge run counter to inveterate habit and prejudice. To assist the process of acceptance, where the workers in the welfare field would really take possession of what is new in our emerging image of the world—this should be the second immediate objective to the educational process. Only then can we think of preparing people to initiate the transmission of new patterns of behavior—by living example, not by preaching in the society at large.

In short, workers in the welfare field will have to go on with what they are doing today, only with a better awareness of the character of the transition which we are approaching. They will have to prepare themselves for the task of being one of the first outposts in the tremendous general reorientation of education toward autonomous self-education of everybody throughout his or her lifetime. And, last but not least, they will have to organize for social action toward the establishment of minimum welfare standards, toward the independent and interdependent functioning of the welfare services throughout the world. The idea that a profession has to be "neutral" in the fundamental questions regarding its activity is one of the rules of every power system, where power to decide the really important interest questions should be concentrated in the hands of the power holders. All others, including those most interested in the issue, are expected to keep their hands off the game.

Assigning this piece of mystification together with many others to where it belongs, the museum of outlived prejudices, we must ask ourselves who is in a better position, more called upon to act collectively, politically, and responsibly for the goals of welfare than those who call welfare their profession and have made it the dominant occupation of their lives.

SOCIAL WELFARE AS A HUMAN RIGHT

*Wayne Vasey**

IT WOULD be a serious mistake to misread the wholesale condemnation of public welfare today. The criticisms are not directed
at the efficiency of the welfare system. They are challenges to the
nature of the institution itself. In other words, it is not a question of
trying to make what we have work better. More precisely, it is a
demand for new approaches, new policies, and new programs which
respond to needs arising out of the massive changes taking place
in our society today.

These challenges are related to the entire social welfare system,
private as well as public. At least, this is what I read in the protest
which is mounting in intensity and which is becoming increasingly
extensive. It is small comfort that the attacks are not limited to the
welfare sector. When the history of the 1960's is written, this baffling
decade may well be known as a period of shocking social discovery—

*Wayne Vasey is a professor at the School of Social Work, University of Michigan,
Ann Arbor, Michigan.

as a time when the rights of many people in the United States were perceived as denied or subverted by the inadequacies of the institutions designed to serve them, not by willful or calculated acts of tyranny or repression.

This has come as a dismal revelation to many of us, especially to those of us who are products of the liberal tradition of the 1930's and who literally grew up professionally in the programs developed in that tradition. We have known that our institutions are not perfect, but we have thought that housing, education, employment services, health services, and welfare would improve, sometimes slowly and at other times rapidly, to the point that they would fulfill their original promise. In the light of recent history, it is rather ironic that more than four and one-half decades ago the late Howard Odum wrote: "Public welfare may be the last and the perfecting stage in an effective democracy."[1] Now, caught between what former Health, Education, and Welfare Secretary John Gardner has termed the "uncritical lovers" who would resist change, and the "unloving critics" who would settle for nothing short of complete demolition, the question is whether social welfare, like other institutions, will survive the onslaught.

Chorus of Condemnation

Conservatives, liberals, and radicals; social scientists, business leaders, labor leaders, and social workers, all lend their voices to the chorus of condemnation. It must be noted, however, that the consensus of criticism is not matched by a corresponding agreement on what should be provided. While some advocate sweeping measures of change toward liberalization of treatment, others concurrently push for rigid measures of control of those receiving public aid. While some speak of basic reforms in our correctional system, others, in the name of law and order, want sterner measures. The struggle between the liberal forces of treatment and the advocates of control is waged on a continuing battleground in many of our social programs. This was never better illustrated than in our public welfare program. At the same time that voices have been raised in favor of national minimum standards, guaranteed minimum income, or

---

[1] Howard W. Odum, "Newer Ideals of Public Welfare," *The Annals of the American Academy of Political and Social Science,* Vol. CV (Jan., 1923), p. 2

family allowances with increasing support, we have had the harsh, repressive features of the welfare provisions of the social security amendments of 1967. Compulsory work and training programs, control over expenditures of funds, and other parts of our welfare program reflect a continuing, debilitating inconsistency.

Our policies today—and in the past as well—are often a reflex of frustration rather than a carefully thought out, well-designed program of action. We are perfectly capable, as the 1967 amendments demonstrate, of combining liberal measures with control features of a most restrictive nature. In part, this grows out of the fact that we have never outlived our history of charity as a theme in social welfare. With such inconsistencies, with our continuing belief that people who are unfortunate are most likely unworthy, we find it easy to convert the tools of benevolence into instruments of control. When welfare loads are increasingly made up of racial or ethnic minorities, they attract special kinds of censure. It is frequently found quite convenient to don the mask of pious disapproval of behavior, real or alleged, to conceal the ugly face of prejudice.

This phenomenon is not limited in its application to the behavior of the poor and disadvantaged. It is my conviction that the concepts of human rights have, at best, a tenuous hold on the hearts and minds of men. Even in societies which profess the highest degrees of belief in the rights of others, there seems to be a pressure point at which human rights cannot be left to the vagaries of current opinion. The thin line that so often separates unconventional from intolerable behavior makes the need acute for a universal standard of human rights which does not apply selectively to class, condition, or race. When people compound the sin of being different by the sin of being poor, they are especially vulnerable to abridgment of their rights.

When the day arrives that our respect for another's rights transcends our disapproval of his behavior or appearance, when color of skin, style of dress, or manner of living are truly "constitutional irrelevancies," our institutions will enlarge, rather than constrict, the domain of human rights. We have never attained this condition. Discrimination in many forms, from the most subtle to the most obvious and blatant, has always been present in American life. Throughout our history, our belief in human rights has been inexorably related to the measure of our attitude toward the person claiming those rights. Unless we have liked him or approved of him, we haven't been too concerned over whether his rights were being threatened.

Human Rights, Not Charity

Apparently in our society, as in others, rights accrue to persons or groups powerful enough to claim them. It is the realization of this fact that has led to pressures for neighborhood control, maximum feasible participation in our poverty programs, the development of welfare rights groups, and other organized efforts to develop political power. Human rights are not a charity. They must be vested, not conferred, and they must be claimed before they can be vested.

Whether or not clearly enunciated, realization of this fact is in back of the militancy which today is being faced by welfare agencies. However harsh or abrasive their behavior may be, these advocates from the ranks of the disadvantaged are demonstrating a realization of what the late Adlai Stevenson once declared was a continuing, unremitting struggle to create a condition in which man could "maintain his dignity and exercise his free and responsible choice."[2]

What the struggles of disadvantaged people show today is what Dr. Odum once called "the inequality of equality of opportunity," which he stated would likely become "the dominant characteristic" of American life unless there was developed a definite "organization and technique" to take care of evolution and change.[3]

We can scarcely claim to have developed an "organization and technique" in social welfare which would serve such a purpose. In fact, our welfare system has been charged with having the opposite effect. It is alleged to have helped to foster inequality, to widen the distance among economic classes, between black and white, between the city ghetto and the prosperous suburbs. By limiting the amounts of our assistance grants, by investigatory practices that invade the privacy of recipients, by challenging the veracity of people receiving aid, by restrictions upon freedom of movement, we have in the past

---

[2] From "The Essence of Democracy: Its Prespects Around the World," quoted in Herbert J. Muller, *Adlai Stevenson: A Study in Values* (New York: Harper and Row, 1967), p. 316.

[3] Odum, *op. cit.,* p. 2.

in this largest of our public welfare programs negated the affirmative hope which motivated the framers of the Social Security Act.

Invoking the Constitution

Fortunately, the courts have stepped into this area with a series of decisions which have brought welfare measures within the range of the Constitution. They have declared that maximum grants are inconsistent in some states where actions have been brought. Two U. S. Supreme Court decisions—both of fundamental importance— promise basic changes in welfare laws. In *King vs. Smith* (#949, 36, U. S. L. W., 1294, Jan. 23, 1968), the U. S. Supreme Court declared unconstitutional the Alabama law denying aid to families of dependent children in which there was a presumptive father, the infamous "man in the home" provision. In *Shapiro vs. Thompson* (#813, 36, U. S. L. W. 3278), the Supreme Court had before it an appeal from a lower court decision declaring state residency laws to be abridgements of the right to travel. Other court decisions have challenged the rights of administrative agencies to establish maximums below needed standards in assistance grants, to terminate aid without administrative hearings, to require divorce or legal separation as a precondition to receiving aid, or to deny assistance to children born out of wedlock.

The development of legal services in advocacy programs for the poor has had a sharp impact. After all, cases must be brought to court before they can be adjudicated. The problems of the legal rights of the poorest of the poor have been made a matter of public record and concern. To welfare administrators, I would say that no administrative agency has yet been created that could, through its own workings, insure constant and inevitable justice under the law. As Charles Reich has reminded us:

> Above all, the time has come for us to remember what the framers of the Constitution knew so well—that 'a power over a man's subsistence amounts to a power over his will.' We cannot safely entrust our livelihoods and our rights to the discretion of authorities, examiners, boards of control, character committees, regents or license commissioners. We cannot permit an official or agency to pretend to sole knowledge of the public good. We cannot put the independence of any man . . . wholly within the power of other men.[4]

---

[4] Charles A. Reich, "Midnight Welfare Searches and the Social Security Act," *Yale Law Journal*, Vol. 72, No. 7 (1963).

Even more important than the individual decision, it seems to me, is the fact that the rights of the poor have been brought within the purview of the Constitution, especially into the Supreme Court of the United States. As Lord Bryce stated many years ago, the Constitution is "the conscience of the people who have resolved to restrain themselves from hasty or unjust action by placing the representatives under the restriction of a permanent law. It is the guarantee of the minority, who, when threatened by the impatient vehemence of a majority, can appeal to this permanent law, finding the interpreter and enforcer thereof in a Court set high above the assaults of factions."[5]

The fact that the Constitution has been invoked to protect the rights of poor people in public housing and in civil law to safeguard the legal rights of children and in the far-reaching Gault decision to apply the Due Process clause of the Fourteenth Amendment of the U. S. Constitution should be cause for gratification to all who believe that the Constitution is a document for all the people, not just for some.

Potent Force of Discrimination

But our pleasure should be tempered by the extent to which rights are still abridged or denied in many places to many people. Racial discrimination in both its most blatant and subtle forms is still a potent force in our society. In 1967 poverty was disproportionately distributed. The ranks of the 33 million poor in this country included 14.3 million children, 6.5 million who were poor because of the inability of the head of the household to work, American Indians living on reservations, Negroes wherever they lived, impoverished farmers, Puerto Ricans, and Mexican Americans in the Southwest. The list of the poor includes many who are working, some employed and underpaid, some who are underemployed. The growing tension between the employed with marginal incomes and the poor receiving aid is one of the disquieting facts in our society today, as well as one of its most threatening features.

Inequality and poverty cover the entire spectrum of age. They

[5] *The American Commonwealth,* as quoted by Eugene V. Rostow in "The Supreme Court and the People's Will," in *Notre Dame Lawyer,* Vol. XXXIII (1958), pp. 579–580.

include babies born into families suffering from the grossest forms of hunger and malnutrition, as revealed by the latest disclosures of hunger in the U. S. There were, in 1967, 700,000 young people between the ages of 16 and 21 who were unemployed and not in school, not to mention those working in dead-end jobs. Poverty among the aged is the most pronounced of all in terms of proportion of the total population.

The mentally and physically disabled may suffer abridgment of their rights in the name of protection. Commitment of the mentally ill to custodial care without opportunity for hearings or adequate review is certainly one such area.

This is a complicated problem for social workers. In our efforts to protect vulnerable people like the mentally ill from the harshness of the adversary process in formal hearings, have we unintentionally aided and abetted arbitrary commitments to custody? When do special measures for protection of the most vulnerable interfere with such human rights as freedom to move in the community? Or opportunity to live up to the limit of one's capacity in the regular life of the society? It is possible to say, of course, that professional judgment is the crucial variable, and that arbitrary deprivation of rights occurs only when such judgment is not available. I wish that I could be sure of this.

This complicated question of human rights could be extended to the problem of the patient in the mental hospital who remains there because of the lack of community facilities rather than because of his specific need for continuing custody and care, to the delinquent in a correctional institution who is denied parole because of the lack of facilities for supervision, to the mentally retarded who remain in institutions because society has not developed other ways of providing opportunities for life outside. I cannot resist adding to this list the old person who remains in a hospital or nursing home because of the lack of social resources for care more related to his capacities for social living.

These and other problems are both individual and class phenomena. The incidence of mental illness is highest among low-income groups, as a number of writers have pointed out. Deprivation of people living in poverty, with poor health care and poor nutrition, may create personal handicaps.

The solutions involve legislation, formal policies, and other decisions which must be made in the context of society itself. But it also reaches into the bureaucratic structure of services. The solutions, however, involve more than bureaucratic reform. They require more than the existence of services—they also demand access to those social services. In public welfare, it means a reorientation from keeping people out to bringing them in when there is legitimate need.

Need for Adequate Theory

I believe, however, that the greatest need today is for a theory adequate to the problems and conditions of our drastically changed society. Incremental improvements and extensions of the present program will not meet the tests of adequacy, decency, and availability. Over the years, as Elizabeth Wickenden has noted, "In our typically pragmatic American fashion, we have borrowed from older countries many traditional forms of social protection and have improved, as our own needs and circumstances demanded, new devices of mutual support to meet specific problems."[6]

In his comments as chairman of the Commission on the Year 2000 of the American Academy, Daniel Bell has called for a new political theory. He has asked, "Can one write a new political theory (descriptive and normative) that deals with a service state and a society characterized by a new mixture of individual and communal —public and private—decision-making units?"[7]

In the more specific context of social welfare, Richard Titmuss has written, "We shall need to shift the emphasis from poverty to inequality, from ad hoc programmes to integrated social rights, from economic growth to social growth."[8]

In this twentieth anniversary year of the adoption of the Universal Declaration of Human Rights by the United Nations Assembly, social welfare could find the basis for a theory adequate for the

---

6 Elizabeth Wickenden, "Social Welfare Law, The Concept of Risk and Entitlement," *University of Detroit Law Journal,* Vol. 43, p. 517.

7 Daniel Bell, "Toward the Year 2000: Work in Progress," *Daedalus,* Summer, 1967, p. 699.

8 Richard Titmuss, *Commitment to Welfare* (New York: Pantheon Books, Random House, 1968), p. 164.

demands of our times. In this declaration the U. N. General Assembly affirmed a belief in the dignity vested in the individual human being wherever he lives, in whatever culture, under whatever condition. It was a ringing declaration of principle; it reflects a standard of aspiration rather than of achievement, but a level of aspiration which could be reflected in the policies of social welfare.

The Universal Declaration included economic, social, and cultural, as well as political and civil, rights. Who more than the people engaged in service in social welfare should recognize the validity of this scope of rights? Under the conditions of today, with the overwhelming influence on the individual of institutions over which he has little, if any, personal control, it becomes imperative that we recognize the necessity for humanizing our service institutions.

Perhaps this is what Dr. Odum, with amazing presence, anticipated in his article 45 years ago when he wrote of the problems of reaching with our democratic ideals and laws "the unequal places and the unequal folk." It is what modern social scientists mean when they refer to the necessity of equality of condition before equality of opportunity can have any significance.

New Relation between Human Rights and Social Welfare

The relation between human rights and social welfare must be more than a casual linkage. The primary mission of our welfare institutions must be one of serving in the front line of the battle to reduce inequality in this society.

It is easier to find the rhetoric for such a philosophy than to explicate the method by which such a purpose can be achieved. As I have struggled with this question, I have found it easy to soar into stratospheric flights of theoretical abstraction or to commit the equally dangerous error of reducing the idea to a list of specifics. The difficulty probably comes from the fact that, while the principle of human rights may be constant, the application of that principle will vary with social conditions. At the risk of sounding too general, I would state that the primary mission of social welfare today is to work on behalf of the most vulnerable members of our society for a condition in which they will have not only material benefits but also the right to enjoy them with security. It means helping these most vulnerable persons to achieve the opportunity to participate fully in the political, social, and economic life of this society. It strongly suggests the extension to all of the protections and privileges afforded by law. It means a genuine right of access to education, to training, and to decent jobs. It means the absence of restraints upon freedom of movement and choice when such restraint is based upon inadequate resources rather than individual need. It means, above all, a commitment to human services as a matter of the highest priority.

In order to be effective in helping to achieve such a condition in such a society, a change in the orientation of social work is required. We must stop putting so much of our energy into attempting to humanize programs which are essentially inhumane. This, I believe, has been the basic error of much of our service approach in public welfare. We must recognize the fact that in any society gross inequality of conditions and severe deprivation for any of the people is unfortunate—in a society like ours it is intolerable.

It is no accident that social workers have been perceived by ghetto dwellers and other disadvantaged folk as creatures of a hostile establishment. Over the years our loyalties have been forged in the functions of the programs in which we have been involved and in the organizations which have administered these programs. To the extent that we have limited our perspective to incremental changes within the limits of these programs we have restricted our effectiveness as forces for real and necessary change. Unless we can shift our perspective to one of primary concern for the overwhelming problems of "unequal folk," we shall find ourselves relegated to the unenviable role of residual caretakers of hopelessness.

There are many pressures against such a change in orientation. Perhaps it isn't so much a change as it is an increasing emphasis on an approach which many social workers have upheld for years—a shift to advocacy as a dominant theme. I do not agree with our harshest critics who allege that we have concealed from the public the unpleasant realities in the lives of our clientele. But I must accept as valid the charge that we have not put enough of our energies into advocacy of more just and effective social programs.

Perhaps the day will come when we can turn our attention exclusively to the problems of individual maladjustment. But now the continued denial of human rights is such a dominant and shocking fact that I see no choice but to apply a large proportion of our energies to the advocacy of change. In this effort we join the ranks of social scientists, civic leaders, industrialists, political leaders, and many others who are speaking the language of change even though they have not found a technology to bring it about. The focal point for our efforts might well be in maximizing the capacity of disadvantaged groups to work for change in their own behalf. New technologies are needed. But overall we must be aware of the fact that this society is involved in a grim race—the race between social justice and social disruption.

STUDENT WISDOM AND VALUES: THE POSITIVE FORCE OF DISAFFECTION

Ernest F. Witte*

THE DISCUSSION of student wisdom and values as presented in this paper is based on the expressed concerns of students with our society and its institutions. Values are represented by the ideals and goals which students, through their actions, have shown they wish to achieve. Wisdom lies in the discretion and judgment reflected in their concerns, in the causes they have chosen, and in the persistence of their efforts to achieve their goals.

The concerns, activities, and accomplishments of social work students, the main focus of this paper, can best be seen against the background of the larger student protest movement, which has been extensively reported and interpreted. Certain of the accounts have been prepared by scholars of considerable standing and provide information not only on the current situation, but also give an historial perspective which is helpful for understanding, although, in

*Ernest F. Witte is dean of the College of Social Professions, University of Kentucky, Lexington, Kentucky.

the end, the reader in view of conflicting judgments must form his own opinions based upon his own experiences.

The Beginnings of Discontent

There is little doubt that students were unhappy and concerned about developments on university campuses and in the country for a considerable period before the public became aware of their discontent. Dr. Harold Taylor suggests that:

> In the latter years of the 1950's a new generation of young people became alive to the reality of social injustice in America by seeing before their eyes members of their own generation beaten by police, goaded by cattle prods, brutalized by police, jailed, and, in some cases, killed. This was advertised to us in a national report, in news media, and on television, and in that time a new attitude was generated in the younger generation which has carried over into contemporary history.[1]

There is general agreement, of course, that the growing involvement of the United States in the war in Vietnam in this period became the crucial issue for students, not only as an issue in itself, but because it heightened their awareness of other issues, especially those of civil rights and racism. In any case, the event that made the nation fully aware of the so-called student "uprising or revolt" took place in the fall of 1964 on the campus of one of our most respected institutions, the Berkeley Campus of the University of California. Dr. Lewis S. Feuer, in describing the "student uprising" at Berkeley says:

> Its story is one of the usual dualities which have characterized student movements: selfless idealism matched with ugly hatreds of generational revolt, high moral ends and low immoral means, a vision of utopian community and a reality of destruction, a populist yearning joined with an elitist self-assertion. Within two years the student movement, which began with an avowal of non-violence and a higher ethic, was becoming the apologist for violence and political amorality.[2]

[1] Dr. Harold Taylor, "Student Unrest—What Students Are Seeking," a National Educational Radio address as broadcast over the University of Kentucky station on November 23, 1969. Student concerns with the foreign policy of John Foster Dulles in the Eisenhower Administration and with certain domestic policies of the same period are also described in this address.

[2] Lewis S. Feuer, The Conflict of Generations (New York: Basic Books, Inc., 1969), p. 436.

A somewhat different point of view is suggested by Dr. Houston Smith, Professor of Philosophy at the Massachusetts Institute of Technology, who, in discussing some of the tactics employed by students, says:

> These are serious defects, but the list of student virtues is at least as long. Studies have shown student activists to be, on the whole, (a) at the better universities, (b) among the better students at these universities, (c) guided by self-accepted moral principles instead of conventional ones or none at all, and (d) in rebellion not against their parents or authority in general but against specific social failings. University of Chicago sociologist M. Brewster Smith summarizes the evidence as follows: 'Student protest is a manifestation of strong moral concern on the part of intelligent and sensitive young people.'[3]

The Causes of Dissent

Student dissent (or rebellion, if you prefer) is indeed one form of value judgment on our universities and the society of which they are a part. My summary of the broad issues which have given rise to dissent would include the following:

1. The goals and values that should guide the nation.

Dissenting students question the concern for material achievements while they see as urgent and necessary a national goal to resolve major social and environmental problems. Students wonder at the failure to deal effectively with racism. They ponder the proportion of governmental resources devoted to war, defense, and explorations of space as contrasted to the amounts made available for environmental improvement, for health services, for the elimination of poverty, for education, and the control of population growth.

2. The hypocrisy which they perceive in so many areas of our society.

The Constitution proclaims a set of values cherished through the years as the foundation of our democratic society. Yet, after some 180 years, a substantial part of our citizenry is still denied the rights held to be universal in this document.

---

[3] Houston Smith, "Like It Is: The University Today," *The Key Reporter*, Winter, 1968-69, p. 4.

We proclaim the brotherhood of man but do not practice it. Even religious institutions, which are founded on this premise, all too often demonstrate that either their members have no understanding of these words or have no commitment to them in practice. We assert that ours is a democratic society, but we don't make it so. We profess concern for the dignity of man, but for millions among us these words have no meaning in reality. We promise a just and equitable society for all when the evidence clearly indicates that this is an unkept promise and one, it appears, we have no will to fulfill.

The society expresses concern because of the alienation of its young people, but it has generally resisted lowering the voting age and all too often offers them token participation in the making of decisions that crucially affect their lives and their future.

In short, concerned students perceive that those who wield the influence and power tend to profess one set of values but live by another set.

3. The complacency of "the university establishment" with existing conditions and the difficulty of arousing sufficient concern to bring about needed change.

Students, especially in larger universities, have been and are all too often treated impersonally, too often find their classes conducted by graduate teaching assistants, and are confronted with a curriculum, a substantial part of which is outdated or otherwise inadequate. They have few opportunities for personal contacts with faculty and find themselves caught in a maze of rules and regulations (many of them arbitrary and administered by clerks), with little provision for them to participate in decisions or to have their opinions seriously considered.

Many students have protested the willingness of universities to lend their facilities and talent in support of war, to engage in (often secret) research to invent more effective means of destruction, and to allow faculty to undertake activities which appear to benefit themselves and the institution, often to the neglect of their direct service to students.

It is more than a little disconcerting to read a current New York State report which says:

The staff director of a state study on campus unrest said today that testimony to the group by college officials had failed to show a deep and abiding concern about student education.

Except for a few, most college administrators are more concerned about buildings, administration, institutes, and programs than about involving the students in the educational process, according to Lloyd L. Hogan, the executive director of the Temporary State Commission to Study Campus Unrest.[4]

There are, of course, numerous other issues that students have raised, but the more universal ones, as far as I can ascertain, lie in the three areas that I have suggested.

Moral Issues of War, Racism, and Poverty

However, there are also specific issues of immediate concern to students which seems more pervasive as judged by their activities both on and off the university campuses. These are:

1. The war in Vietnam.

Many students tend to identify whatever they regard as wrong in the society as somehow reflected in this undeclared war. Certainly we can all admit that it is a war in which we had little excuse for becoming involved. It has become one of the most divisive issues in our society and its corruptive influences on our institutions and upon our democratic and social aspirations will be with us for many long years to come.

In substantial measure we have university students to thank for arousing the country to the iniquity of this war, for helping the public understand its impact and significance for our society, for developing pressures for terminating our involvement, and for making clear to faculty and administrative officers that they cannot ignore the moral issues which are involved in the way they have allowed their institutions to become partners in what many students consider an immoral enterprise. To suggest, as some have, that student interest in this issue is simply self-serving is a gross misrepresentation. Many of them have shown their dedication to the principles they believe should govern our international relations by the courage they have

---

4 *New York Times,* November 27, 1969.

shown in opposing the war and the punishment they have had to take as a result.[5]

James Kunen, a Columbia University student, has, I think, emphasized the value issue of this situation by asking: "Isn't it singular that no one ever goes to jail for waging wars, let alone for advocating them, but the jails are filled with those who want peace?"[6]

2. Racism.

Students perhaps as much or more than any other group in our country have recognized the social cancer of racism which continues to be so pervasive among us. It has been students who have exposed racism on campuses and who have been persistent and insistent on its elimination in many places.[7] That they have not always acted wisely in the methods used to eliminate this social infection is hardly surprising. The fact that their efforts have not been more successful, particularly in eliminating racism in our universities, only suggests the depth and the difficulty of the problem.

Nor have students been satisfied with the general disclaimer of university administrations that they have neither the means nor the responsibility to fight racism in the general community. Student pressure has led some universities to new and promising ways to force changes which affect both on-campus and off-campus practices in, for example, the training and employment of larger numbers of minority employees in construction work. We need more such efforts on all campuses.

---

[5] The Urban Research Corporation, in reporting on its study of some 122 campus disturbances in the first six months of 1969, states that 22% of these protests were related to the war in Vietnam but very few of the protests related to the draft or called for an end of the war. The Lexington (Kentucky) *Herald*, January 15, 1970, "69 Protests Centered on Black Issues."

[6] James Kunen, *The Strawberry Statement—Notes of a College Revolutionary* (New York: Random House, 1968), p. 61.

[7] The Urban Research Corporation reports that 44% of 232 colleges it surveyed were affected by student demands during the first six months of 1969, and that black students were involved in more than half of them, although they constituted only 6% of the student population. Racism was the major issue in nearly half of these student disturbances. There was no violence or destruction in 76% of these protests. The Lexington (Kentucky) *Herald*, January 1, 1970, *op. cit.*

3. The elimination of poverty.

Students know that as a nation we have the resources to lift everyone out of the poverty level but that we have not mustered the will to do so. They know, too, that this issue is related to other inequities in our national, as well as the world, society. The direct participation of students in poverty programs has made a tremendous contribution to the results as well as providing them with meaningful learning opportunities. We expect social work students to be involved, but I have been particularly impressed, as you doubtless have been, with the significant interest and participation in programs designed to eliminate poverty by many students from other fields, especially students in law, architecture, and, to a lesser extent, in medicine. They have not only provided services to the poor but have had an impact upon the attitude and action of the professional associations in their fields.

Impact of Student Action

Despite the fact that critics generally argue that universities have not responded to the pressures for change as the need for change demands and that some university officials may not be as responsive as they should be, substantial changes have occurred which will become more apparent as time goes on. Undoubtedly, there will be additional changes as a result of past and continuing student action. In the main, these are important changes which will improve our institutions of higher education.

For one thing, university officials are now much more sensitive to student suggestions. When before have university students been members of so many governing boards, been allowed and invited to attend and participate in faculty senate meetings, been consulted on policy decisions before they are made, served on the selection committees for top-level university officials, or been invited to participate in the evaluation of faculty? When have campus publications been so free or used their freedom to discuss so many critical and sensitive issues? University officials are more concerned than they have been for some time about the quality of instruction, the way faculty use their time, and with the quality of the counseling and advising services provided students.

The impact which students have made, and are continuing to make, on institutions of higher learning will profoundly change and, in my opinion, substantially improve them. We need to remind ourselves, however, that changes beget the need for even more change. We are unlikely to reach a period when student activists will be satisfied with the university; if they were, stagnation might become an even greater problem.

Perhaps the aspect that I have admired most among students, many of whom could take the far easier road of conformity, is the courage they have shown. Substantial numbers of them have literally had the courage of their convictions. They may not have differed too much with the values held by their parents, but, unlike many of their parents, they have risked careers, social disapproval, and sometimes life itself, in support of what they believe. This quality should not be overlooked in moments of annoyance with some of their methods or their presumed motives.

I will forego the temptation to try to assess the impact which students may have had up to this time upon society generally. Even if students cease being concerned and active, it would be some years before any such real assessment could be made. But if Houston Smith is right when he says, "Our students are forcing us to face the fundamental issue of how we can get the America we want,"[8] can we expect any more fundamental contribution than this?

Social Work Students

It is my impression that social work students, while generally in agreement with the major objectives of the larger student movement and holding many of the same values, have generally, with few exceptions, been less belligerent and less global in their aspirations than the general body of student activists. They have focused their efforts for change on more specific goals of more immediate and direct concern to them. One must also acknowledge that over periods of time their interests and activities change and shift. For whatever reasons, graduate students generally have been less active than other students. The Lipset-Altbach study makes it clear that majors in the social sciences and humanities appear to be more involved in the student movement than students from other fields. They also indi-

[8]Smith, op. cit., p. 4.

cate that the career goals of student activists are predominantly centered in teaching, social service, and research.[9] In the light of this information, perhaps we may look forward to even more student involvement and militancy in schools of social work in the future.

In a less than complete survey of the professional literature in social work, I have found little that indicates with reasonable certainty what values students bring to schools of social work or what their values are when they leave.[10] Admittedly, it is difficult to find reliable measures of these intangibles. Indeed, I am somewhat uncertain as to the general values held by the social work profession itself.[11] The corroding influence of the materialistic society in which social work is practiced appears to change the behavior and values of social workers and make their response more nearly like that of the general public despite professed goals which would suggest a different pattern.

It is my observation, however, that social work students, at the time they are admitted to schools of social work, have been more idealistic, more concerned to build an equitable society, and more enthusiastic about the potential contributions of social work than they are when they graduate. The reasons for these changes in students may well be the result of a better understanding of the causes of the problems and the difficulties of getting at them than they had when they were admitted. But this may also be the result of uninspired teaching, an undue stress on a given method which offers little promise of getting at basic causes, perhaps too little concern with some of the major problems of our society, such as racism, alienation, the distribution of income, and the challenge of change to the present society.

In our emphasis on current student activity, we should not forget that many social work students have always had a bent for social action. I recall an experience with the wisdom, determination, and power of students in the late thirties, when some members of

[9]Seymour Martin Lipset and Philip G. Altbach, "Student Politics and Higher Education in the United States," *Comparative Education Review*, Vol. 10, No. 2 (June, 1966), p. 332.

[10]See Barbara K. Varley, "Social Work Values: Changes in Value Commitments of Students from Admission to MSW Graduation," *Journal of Education for Social Work*, Vol. 4, No. 2 (Fall, 1968), pp. 67 ff.

[11]See Ruby B. Pernell, "Social Work Values on the New Frontiers," *supra*, p. 44.

the legislature decided to override the decision of the Board of Regents in establishing a school of social work at the University of Nebraska by eliminating the funds requested in the budget for its support. The students of the school, knowing the awkward position of the director of the school in the situation, organized themselves to save it. They did this by skillful organizing and lobbying. They kept a student on the floor of the legislature every moment it was in session and in continuous attendance at every meeting of the Appropriations Committee in order not to be taken by surprise. They had a system of alerts by which in thirty minutes they could mobilize a group of students from the home districts of each of the members of the Appropriations Committee. Some of these students have told me they learned more about effective political action in that undertaking than they ever learned in their seminar on social action.

Nevertheless, there is something different about the attitude, sophistication, and behavior of the social work students of recent years. When I returned to work on a campus approximately seven years ago, I was startled by the contrast with those I had worked with earlier. Doubtless, these changes had begun long before, but I had not become aware of them. The adjustment to the new breed of students was not easy.

An increasing number of our students are married, are parents, are participants in a variety of community activities apart from their roles as students. They are often taxpayers and voters. Many have been abroad as students; some have been members of the Peace Corps. All of this has made a substantial contribution to the change. Many of them are demanding; they want quick action rather than promises; they are critical and outspoken; they openly challenge long-established requirements, regulations, and procedures; and it is not surprising that they soon began to demand as a right participation in making decisions which had earlier been the responsibility of the dean, and, more recently, ones which he had only reluctantly been compelled to share with the faculty.

Dr. Henry Steele Commager has best described this change in students for me as follows:

Students who once went to the university to prepare for a career or, as we amiably say, 'to prepare for life' now find that the university is life. Parents who looked upon the university as a golden interlude before their children faced the hard realities of life are confronted by the fact that college years are not an interlude, but the real thing, and that they are not golden, but iron.[12]

Schools of social work, being a part of the university, have been subject to many of the same deficiencies as exist in the parent institution, although perhaps not to the same degree, since social work education has been more student-focused and less impersonal than higher education in general.

Social work students, it seems to me, have been especially concerned that they have more opportunity to participate meaningfully in all of the activities and decisions of the school. Their reasons for this have been many, including a strong desire to make the institution more democratic, to reduce the sometimes arbitrary or capricious exercise of authority of an individual faculty member or dean over a given student, to change the requirements and curriculum so that students may have more time to pursue some of their own special academic or social work interests, and/or learn more about the social change functions of social work as against the treatment function so generally emphasized in the traditional curriculum. They seek to move the school faculty to become activists in improving welfare services, reforming social institutions, and supporting students in similar efforts.

Let me give a recent example of this new type of involvement. For some time most of us have known how callous our field has been in its failure to provide at least emergency services at night and on weekends, but tradition and inertia are difficult to overcome through persuasion and resolution. In San Diego, students placed in a field unit where they got a clear picture of the circumstances did not stop by presenting the need for such services to the agencies of this city, but themselves established a twenty-four-hour, seven-days-a-week emergency service which they staffed on their own time and publicized through feature stories and broadcasts. They thus demonstrated that there is a legitimate *need* for and *use* of such services and literally forced the public welfare department to institute an emergency service available at times when the agency was normally closed.

Another demand of social work students, not unlike those of other students, is for a closer and more significant relationship with

---

[12]Henry Steele Commager, "The Crisis of the University," in *1970 Information Please Almanac* (New York: Dan Golenpaul Associates, 1969), p. 59.

faculty.[13] This concern of many social work students is a little surprising in view of our perception of ourselves, our schools, and of student-faculty relations. I note that the students with whom I have had contact in recent years have placed increasing emphasis upon the ability and interest of faculty to relate significantly to students. This has been again impressed upon me by *ad hoc* committees of seniors in our social work major in my own university who have interviewed prospective faculty for the graduate program now being developed. They have invariably, and on their own initiative, given priority to the capacity and ability of the prospective faculty member to relate in a meaningful way to them and the evidence of his interest to do so as based upon his record in previous positions.

In this connection, we might ponder the comment of these students to the effect that some faculty applicants seem more interested in the salary, the teaching load, and the fringe benefits offered than they are in the goals and program of the school in which they seek employment and whether it will afford them the opportunity to maximize their potential for service, or what concerns students. The ability of these students to assess qualities of empathy, depth, sincerity, and conviction about social work and student values has been a surprise to some of us and again suggests our tendency to underestimate the capacity of students when they are interested and challenged.

Significance of Student Demands

While the proportion of social work students who might be classified as activists is perhaps relatively small and varies tremen-

[13]This observation would seem to be supported by the following statement:

"One dean emphasized that for the majority of students what really matters is the quality of the relationships between students and faculty. This depends not on contractual papers but on mutual give and take in a dynamic relationship. Given real confidence and adequate communication, this dean felt that policies and procedures were only a means to the end of collaboration—with the formal arrangements changing and evolving all the time to meet the needs of the partners."

See "Some Issues Identified by the Graduate Schools of Social Work Regarding Student Rights and Responsibilities," A Working Paper for Committee on Students discussion, October 13-14, 1969 (doc. #69-350-13), Council on Social Work Education, New York.

dously from school to school, their contribution to social work education generally may well turn out to be successful. So, also, is the benefit that has already begun to accrue to practice. Many of these students have revitalized local chapters of the National Association of Social Workers and their potential impact on the national office itself is perhaps just becoming visible. From among their contributions, which also have a significant national impact through the Council on Social Work Education, let me list the following:

• Their demand that we recruit more students from minority groups. In many instances they have been effective instruments in their recruitment and I hope will be even more so in the future.[14]

• Their demand to participate in all the important planning and decision-making processes of the school and in related social work organizations. This has generally been beneficial and wholesome.

• Their demand for important improvements in the treatment of students. Certainly one immediate outgrowth has been a clarification of student rights and freedom, embodied in documents developed in individual schools and nationally by the Council on Social Work Education.[15] We may yet find it possible to allow students to challenge the accreditation of a school of social work for educational reasons, a suggestion which even a few years ago it was heresy to propose.

[14]See Mary Ella Robertson, "The Role of Students," *Journal of Education for Social Work,* Vol. 4, No. 1 (Spring, 1968), pp. 55 ff.

[15]See (a) Lilian Ripple, "Students' Rights and Responsibilities in Graduate Schools of Social Work: Survey of Current Practice," *Social Work Education Reporter,* Vol. XVI, No. 2 (June, 1969), pp. 48 ff.; (b) Gordon Hearn, "Student Rights and Responsibilities: Issues and Questions" (mimeo), presented at a meeting of deans and directors in January, 1969, Council on Social Work Education; (c) "Joint Statement of Rights and Freedoms of Students," American Association of University Professors *Bulletin,* Winter, 1967, pp. 365 ff.; (d) "Student Records and Release of Information about Students" (mimeo), Council on Social Work Education, September 17, 1969; (e) Mather P. Dumont, M.D., "Young People—A Community Asset" (mimeo), The National Assembly for Social Policy and Development, May 2, 1969; and (f) "Some Issues Identified by the Graduate Schools of Social Work Regarding Student Rights and Responsibilities" (mimeo), Council on Social Work Education, October 13-14, 1969.

• Their clear commitment to career goals of social significance. Many of them find the dedication of this society largely to materialistic goals disappointing and frustrating. Even more disturbing to the service-oriented and idealistic student coming to a school of social work is the influence which the goals and practices of the larger society have upon the values of social work practitioners. (Unfortunately, perhaps their indignation does not always continue after they enter practice and thus sufficiently influence their own subsequent behavior.)

It appears to me that social work students have shown by their demands that they want their educational institutions to be models for what they would like the larger community to be—that is:

• A place where every individual, without regard to race, color, religion, or financial circumstances, has a reasonable opportunity to qualify for admission to a school of social work and, once admitted, to develop his competence for effective performance.

• A place where there is opportunity for all to participate in planning, decision-making, and evaluation of outcome.

• A place where each is assured the right to his opinions, the right to express them without fear of penalty, and the assurance that they will be considered.

• A place where individual dignity and human values are recognized in the quality of the relationships established among all those directly involved in the educational process.

• A place where emphasis is given to the obligation for service above that placed upon the enhancement of the profession.

• A place which understands and accepts the responsibilities for helping to develop and maintain an equitable and livable society in which the university is an integral part and for which it has a major responsibility.

• A place where education is kept abreast of changing circumstances so that graduates are as effectively equipped to cope with the needs of today and tomorrow as the state of the knowledge and the art permits.

- A place and a profession in which there is a focus not only upon helping the damaged members of our society but where attempts are made to prepare students for coping more effectively with the circumstances which contribute to the number who are so damaged.
- A place where civil rights and privacy are respected.

We are all familiar with these objectives and the values they represent. They are our goals, too. The fact that students have become more militant in support of these objectives and want to share more fully and actively in their achievement is gratifying. That they want to modify the structure, processes, and education provided in our schools in order that the results of our efforts may be more consistent with these objectives may create some temporary problems, but we must generally applaud their judgment for their effort to move us in this direction.

There are, of course, a number of difficult questions involved in how students can make their maximum contributions in helping schools achieve these goals. Some of these problems have been set forth cogently in a CSWE "Working Paper for Discussion by the Committee on Students."[16] Since students and faculty have mutual goals, finding acceptable ways for resolving these issues should not prove insurmountable. In a partnership, which is what education should be, both partners have equal responsibilities as well as rights if it is to work successfully. Partners should neither attempt to intimidate one another nor allow themselves to be intimidated, and both must always be open for discussion, irrespective of the issues raised.

In this connection I would like to quote from an earlier lecture in this memorial series made by Eugen Pusic in which he states:

> Education generally, assuming paramount importance as the process of self-programming human behavior, cannot remain what it has been: a process of imparting knowledge and conditioning behavior performed by one group of people upon another group. The fundamental premises of this relationship of subjects to objects of the teaching operation are no longer tenable. It is equally obvious that education cannot be limited to any particular part of the life cycle. . . . Understanding change and social development, a 'feel' for the problems inherent in the various development situations cannot be taught

[16]"Some Issues Identified by the Graduate Schools of Social Work Regarding Student Rights and Responsibilities," A Working Paper for Committee on Students discussion, October 13-14, 1969, Council on Social Work Education, New York.

at all in the traditional sense. This can be acquired only by the learner autonomously in discussion and observation.[17]

Concluding Remarks

I am well aware that my enthusiasm for the contributions students have made in bringing dramatically to our attention the inequities in our universities, schools, and the larger community and the need for reform and change, will not be shared by everyone. I could, if any purpose were served, point out negatives in the so-called "student rebellion" of recent years. Certainly there have been inconsistencies in their complaints and assertions, arrogant and unreasonable demands have been made, dissent and disruption have on occasion been ends in themselves, unnecessary violence has sometimes been resorted to, and, in the words of John Galbraith, I deplore the "unwillingness of so many to engage in the process of thought, study, and reflection before they pontificate on great social issues,"[18] a characteristic, of course, that is not confined to students. In my opinion, negatives are present in any significant movement, but the positive contributions of students have greatly outweighed the negatives. The frequent charge that students have no program seems a bit specious to me. They may not have produced the means for effecting the changes they have suggested are needed, but who among us has?

I am aware, also, that a favorite interpretation of the student disaffection is the psychoanalytic one that it is the more or less traditional rebellion against parental authority.[19] Doubtless this may be involved, but there is more to it than this and, whatever the reason, let us not overlook the validity of the issues raised. It was the Secretary of Health, Education, and Welfare who said in an interview with the Washington *Post* that American Universities are probably "more rigid than almost any other institution in our society . . . in the face

[17]Pusic, *supra*, p. 60.

[18]As quoted by Ernest F. Witte in "A World We Never Made," in *Social Work Promises and Pressures*, Sue Spencer, ed. (Nashville: The University of Tennessee, 1968), p. 32.

[19]See E. A. Rubenstein, "Paradoxes of Student Protests," *American Psychologist*, Vol. 24 (1969), pp. 133–141, and subsequent issues for comments.

of very fast changing conditions."[20]

Some of the views I have expressed regarding our institutions of higher learning and the society in which we live have been rather negative. This is not to suggest that there are no positives, for, of course, there are many, as the following examples will serve to make clear:

> The fact that our universities can be centers of conflict and controversy is, in itself, a tribute and one which we must not overlook. There are other countries and other systems where this is not permitted.
>
> Where else but America would such a large proportion of young people be afforded an opportunity for a university education, or such large sums invested in providing the resources necessary to make this possible?
>
> Where else in time of war are there so many legal safeguards, despite their imperfections, to protect the right of criticism and of protest?
>
> And despite our disappointments and frustrations over the lack of adequate funding and public support, our government is on record officially as determined to eliminate poverty and racism. Ours is the task of motivation to see that these promises are carried out.

These positives and many others are worth preserving and, if the criticisms sound negative, it is only because our students and we know there is both a great need and adequate means to make ours a better society.

Charles Morgan, head of the American Civil Liberties Union Regional Office, has sounded an alert by suggesting:

> It is not by great acts but by small failures that freedom dies. The sense of justice dies slowly in a people. They grow used to the unthinkable and sometime they may look back and begin to wonder when things changed. Justice and liberty die quietly because men first learn to ignore injustice and then no longer recognize it.[21]

---

20 As quoted by Ernest F. Witte in "Prevention—The Shadow Area of Social Work" (mimeo), Veterans Administration Forum, Salt Lake City, May 16, 1969.

21 As quoted in Lexington (Kentucky) Sunday *Herald-Leader* in the article, "United States Turned Corner Sometime During Violent and Baffling 1960's," p. 78.

Let us say to ourselves of our students, as an Englishman said to his countrymen soon after 1776:

> Strong mother of the lion line,
> Be proud of these strong sons of thine
> Who wrenched their rights from thee.[22]

I hope I have not violated in this presentation the philosophy, the values, or the wisdom of the colleague in whose honor it is made. Betty Neely was a colleague whom we loved and respected because of the values she both held and lived by, the innate wisdom she exemplified in her own life, and her respect and enthusiasm for students with whom she shared a kindred spirit of the possible, which they help to perpetuate among us.

---

[22]Tennyson, "England and America, 1782," as quoted by Houston Smith, "Like It Is: The University Today," *op. cit.,* p. 4.

A COLLEAGUE'S TRIBUTE

Katherine A. Kendall*

THE CHOICE of a theme for the Ann Elizabeth Neely lectures posed no problem for the committees of friends who launched the memorial series. It was axiomatic that a lecture series in her honor should deal with social justice, human rights, and social values within the context of education for social work.

In many respects, Betty Neely was a symbol of a simpler age. In her personal life and professional career, she personified values that in her professional lifetime were clearly accepted as the central core of social work. All of her adult years were given fully, joyously, and without stint to the service of others. She believed in the mission and contribution of social work as a helping profession and as a force for social change. She is remembered not so much for great tangible achievements—although they are there to admire—but rather for her genius in human relationships.

*Katherine A. Kendall is director of International Education at the Council on Social Work Education and secretary general of the International Association of Schools of Social Work.

When Betty Neely died in October, 1966, there were shadows on the land that gave warning of trouble to come. But the age of discontent so tellingly revealed in this memorial volume had not yet taken shape. The central theme of values, chosen in the first instance as a particularly appropriate tribute to a woman of rare spirit and great humanity, now takes on a more profound significance because of doubts about the existence or worth of the values that traditionally have been attributed to the social worker.

The papers in the lecture series, each in its own way, raise questions about the relevance of social work values in confronting the new realities of today's world. Each of the authors has laid bare old commitments, sometimes in moving personal testimony and always with lucid arguments. Yet, the message that comes through the memorial lectures is strongly affirmative, pointing to the potential for positive action that resides in social work and social work education.

This message will stand as a fitting memorial to Ann Elizabeth Neely. Although a gentle person, Betty Neely was no stranger to dissent. In a quiet way, she was a persistent fighter for the good that she wanted for everyone, everywhere in the world. And she was an affirmative person, completely incapable of despair or apathy. Her values served as an unerring guide to genuine and meaningful involvement with her fellowmen.

This volume is a memorial to Betty Neely. In the making of a memorial, we may have found that one answer to doubt and uncertainty about the relevance of social work in an age of discontent is to live, as she did, the values we have so long professed.